THE EVERYTHING
Rock & Blues Piano Book

Dear Reader,

The Everything® Rock & Blues Piano Book with CD was a labor of love for me, and I hope that the information found on the following pages will help you grow as a pianist and as a musician. While no book can cover literally *everything* you need to know about a particular subject, I hope this book points you in the right direction. In short, I hope that this book serves you for years to come as a credible reference.

No matter what style of music you play, it's important to keep an open mind. This is the only way to learn. Given this, I hope you'll take some time to listen to the many blues and rock artists mentioned in this book. As I researched this book, I constantly found myself in a state of awe as I listened to pianists like Brother Ray, Dr. John, Pinetop Perkins, Johnnie Johnson, Thelonious Monk, and so many others. I hope you feel the same when you hear these masters play.

In the end, it's not really about books, notation examples, or study pieces. It's about the music *you* make! Therefore, get out there and play. The more time you spend at the piano, the better you will be. Just remember, the piano is only a tool. You must be the craftsperson, the artist, the inventor. Good luck and, as always, rock on.

Eric Alan

The EVERYTHING® Series

Editorial

Publisher	Gary M. Krebs
Director of Product Development	Paula Munier
Managing Editor	Laura M. Daly
Executive Editor, Series Books	Brielle K. Matson
Associate Copy Chief	Sheila Zwiebel
Acquisitions Editor	Lisa Laing
Development Editors	Jessica LaPointe
	Brett Palana-Shanahan
Production Editor	Casey Ebert

Production

Director of Manufacturing	Susan Beale
Production Project Manager	Michelle Roy Kelly
Prepress	Erick DaCosta
	Matt LeBlanc
Interior Layout	Heather Barrett
	Brewster Brownville
	Colleen Cunningham
	Jennifer Oliveira
Cover Design	Erin Alexander
	Stephanie Chrusz
	Frank Rivera

Visit the entire Everything® Series at *www.everything.com*

THE
EVERYTHING®
ROCK
&
BLUES
PIANO
BOOK

Master riffs, licks, and blues styles from New Orleans to New York City

Eric Starr

Adams Media
Avon, Massachusetts

Dedicated to my son, Iain Wesley,
who was born during the writing of this book.

An Everything® Series Book.
Everything® and everything.com® are registered trademarks of F+W Publications, Inc.

Published by Adams Media, an F+W Publications Company
57 Littlefield Street, Avon, MA 02322 U.S.A.
www.adamsmedia.com

ISBN 10: 1-59869-260-7
ISBN 13: 978-1-59869-260-0

Printed in the United States of America.

J   I   H   G   F   E   D   C   B   A

Library of Congress Cataloging-in-Publication Data
Starr, Eric.
The Everything Rock & Blues Piano Book with CD : master riffs, licks,
and blues styles from New Orleans to New York City / Eric Starr.
p. cm. – (The Everything series)
ISBN-13: 978-1-59869-260-0 (pbk.)
ISBN-10: 1-59869-260-7 (pbk.)
1. Piano music (Rock)–Instruction and study. 2. Piano music
(Blues)–Instruction and study. 3. Rock music–Instruction and
study. 4. Blues (Music)–Instruction and study. I. Title.

MT239.S815 2007
786.2'1931643–dc22
2007002721

This book is available at quantity discounts for bulk purchases.
For information, please call 1-800-289-0963.

Contents

Acknowledgments

I would like to thank my acquisitions editor Lisa Laing for asking me to write this book and to the rest of the staff at Adams Media, for believing in this project. I'd also like to thank Marc Schonbrun for his help formatting the book's notation and for supplying lots of "cogent" computer assistance. Also, thanks to Jeffrey Starr for his "proper posture" and "hands pictorial" line art and for installing essential computer software.

Special thanks to Nelson Starr for supplying me with around twenty-five invaluable blues and rock notation examples. Also, special thanks to Charles Freeman for supplying me with a stride piano left-hand pattern. Further, special thanks for Wynn Yamami for proofreading my notation examples. Finally, very special thanks to my wife, Katherine, for her constant support and guidance.

Top Ten Things You'll Learn
from This Book

1. The fundamental elements of the blues including its origins, development, and global influence.

2. The basic elements of rock including its origins and evolution; you will also learn about how rock has changed and morphed since its inception.

3. Essential biographical information on rock and blues piano and keyboard innovators.

4. Key movements and eras in blues and rock from 1900 to 2000 and beyond. You will learn about rock's kinship with the blues.

5. Practical rock and blues licks, riffs, and clichés used by the pros.

6. Music theory: This book details harmony, melody, rhythm, and song structure in a nonclassical, easy-to-follow format.

7. How to simulate the playing styles of key innovators such as Ray Charles, Jerry Lee Lewis, Dr. John, Rick Wakeman, Ray Manzarek, Billy Joel, and many others.

8. Tips for practicing, which will maximize your efficiency and rate of progress.

9. How to purchase the piano or keyboard that is right for you.

10. How to continue your education. This book includes a list of essential media resources (books, Web sites, and videos) you should use to take your playing to the next level.

Introduction

▶ WELCOME TO *The Everything® Rock & Blues Piano Book with CD*! This book is designed to give you an insider's look at rock and blues as it relates to the piano. Moreover, this book will help you grow as a musical conceptualist. In general, this book will teach you what to play, why to play it, and most important, how to play it.

The goal is to unlock the secrets of rock and blues and get you started on the road to musical success. Will you learn everything there is to know about rock and blues from this text? Unfortunately, the answer is no. No publication could ever boast such a thing. Even entire music libraries could never make such claims.

If you wanted to fully understand rock and blues, you would need to immerse yourself in the cultures of these styles. This is true of any musical genre. However, you don't need to *live* rock and blues in order to enjoy it and begin playing it.

The Everything® Rock & Blues Piano Book with CD will start you off on the right foot by rooting you in the history of the blues, which is the parent genre of rock. As you proceed, this book will encourage you to develop your musical ear, your creative mind, and your own musical preferences. It is also hoped that you will feel inspired as you master each new exercise and each new concept.

The table of contents reveals the topics covered in this book. However, the text can be broken down into three main categories:

1. How-to guide
2. Biographical and historical information
3. Resource guide

The Everything® Rock & Blues Piano Book with CD employs beginner to intermediate music reading and beginner to advanced musical concepts. Along the way, every attempt has been made to write in a clear, easy-to-follow manner, and when possible, to write the how-to material in a step-by-step format.

This book assumes that you do not speak the language of music so it provides a crash course on the basics of music notation and piano technique. However, this book ultimately focuses on rock and blues. Therefore, it is not a substitute for a beginner piano method. If you've never touched a piano before, it's recommended that you first work your way through a "Book One" before focusing on the rock and blues material found here. Why? It's important to begin with the basics, the fundamentals of music. This book only reviews them. As the old adage states, "You can't walk before you can crawl."

There is another expression: "No one is an island." This maxim means that no person is separate, alone, or autonomous. Instead, all people are connected by family bonds, cultural ties, national identities, and more.

The same is true of music. In this sense, you could say, "No music is an island." Rock and blues exist as part of a greater development in Western music that traces its origins to European classical and folk music and in the regional music of West Africa. Although rock and blues were born in the United States, they are ultimately part of a greater musical collective. As a result, *The Everything® Rock & Blues Piano Book with CD* examines rock and blues from a global perspective. This perspective attempts to see music through connections and associations, kinships and nexus.

It is hoped that you will examine rock and blues from this same vantage point. If you do, you will open yourself up to the "great conversation" of music, and in the long run, you will learn not just about rock and blues but also about a wide assortment of musical cultures, styles, and ideas.

Along the way, when playing through the musical examples in this book, keep in mind that the tempo (speed) markings are not ironclad; they are merely recommendations. As you practice, feel free to play any of these musical figures slower than indicated to meet your needs.

Chapter 1
Rock and Blues 101

Blues and rock are inextricably connected, and it's not uncommon for musicians to refer to rock as the "child" or "cousin" of the blues. In this chapter, you will explore the roots of both styles and better understand the relationship between the two. You will also begin to learn about the chief innovators of each style.

History of the Blues

Most genres of music are derived from an earlier style or era. The blues is no exception. However, its development is unique. The European model is often used to describe musical progress in the West. In classical, there are essentially eight phases: medieval, renaissance, baroque, classical, romantic, postromantic, modern, and postmodern. The romantic period is the direct result of the classical period. The classical period is the direct result of the baroque period. The baroque period is the direct result of the renaissance, and so on.

FACT

African griot singing influenced the blues the most. Griots are poets and storytellers. Typically, they do not perform in groups but solo. They also accompany themselves on a stringed instrument not unlike the guitar. In many ways, this parallels the approach of the early blues singer.

This suggests that Western music was developed linearly. Each period grew out of an earlier epoch. This occurred in Europe because of musical notation. Notation is a system of cataloging musical ideas through written symbols. These symbols form a language that can be used to store, communicate, and process musical thoughts. Ultimately, notation has made it possible for composers from different eras to interact and communicate with one another on a specific, integrated level.

African Origins

Unlike European music, the blues is rooted in the oral traditions of Africa. Oral traditions revolve around regions, communities, and tribes. These groups of people are not always linked. In fact, they are often independent and detached. For example, it would be rare to find a singer who's directly influenced by a tribe that lives 5,000 miles away. Interaction could occur through migration. However, this would be a slow, gradual process spanning generations.

For the most part, oral societies are localized and their music is distilled from their own community's experiences. Usually, these societies seek to keep the traditions and customs of their people alive through the telling and retelling of stories. Without a doubt, the blues grew out of localized African storytelling traditions. Yet, the blues is wholly American and its attachment to Africa should not be overemphasized. This music was the direct result of colonialism, and it was born on the shores of the New World.

At its root, the blues is the sound of depression, unrest, sorrow, loneliness, discrimination, and heartache. Because it stems from a highly personalized, internal sense of suffering, it ultimately reflects back on itself. Due to its universal themes of love and torment, its lack of pretension, and its infectious use of rhythm, the blues has widespread appeal.

Blues melodies, singing styles, structures, and rhythms can all be traced back to the tribal music of Africa. As far back as the sixteenth century, music from the Congo and Angola regions, Nigeria, Mozambique, Madagascar, and Senegambia filtered into the New World through the slave trade.

American Blues

To understand the blues, you will have to go back to slavery and to the hopelessness of life for black Americans after the Civil War. The promise of freedom—granted to all black people by the Emancipation Proclamation—was tempered by the harsh realities of finding a job and raising a family. In this climate, the blues was born. It is a story of chains, bondage, abuse, and inhumanity. It comes from appalling work conditions on cotton and tobacco plantations and in the timber, turpentine, and levee camps of the Deep South. It is the story of depravity, frustration, helplessness, and unyielding racism.

Blues antecedents came in the form of field hollers, work songs, spirituals, and jump-ups. Field hollers were sung on plantations while tilling the fields or picking cotton. Work songs were structured group songs also sung while working in the fields. Spirituals were early gospel (religious) tunes, and jump-ups were one-verse dance songs. All of these songs were used to combat loneliness, to communicate with others, and to entertain. During the nineteenth century, these singing styles were emulated in minstrel shows, albeit mockingly, and in vaudeville theater acts.

Early Innovators

The Mississippi Delta is considered the birthplace of the blues since it was here that the blues was first documented around 1900. Blues scholars cite Charley Patton (1891–1934) as a central player in the development of the blues. Some even call him the founding father. Clearly, Patton influenced blues legends such as Son House, Robert Johnson, Howlin' Wolf, John Lee Hooker, and a whole host of others. In the 1960s, folk singer Bob Dylan would also come to emulate Patton's style.

FACT

Ragtime is a style of music that uses stride piano techniques and syncopated rhythms. It is also notated, not improvised. Ragtime was influenced by European classical. However, it played a role in the development of jazz. Scott Joplin is the best-known ragtime composer. His piece "Maple Leaf Rag" was published in 1899.

Despite his musical legacy, Patton was not the inventor of the blues. Historians believe that Patton was strongly influenced by a man named Henry Sloan. Little is known about Sloan, except that he probably taught Patton how to play the guitar. It's estimated that Sloan began playing the blues as early as 1897, making him one of the first known blues musicians.

The blues remained confined to the Deep South until the arrival of W. C. Handy (1873–1958). Handy single-handedly transformed the blues from a backwoods style of music to a new form of entertainment that could be bought, sold, and marketed. Handy's blues was informed by the Delta but only in the most indirect of ways. Songs such as "Memphis Blues," "St. Louis Blues," and "Beale Street Blues" were influenced more by ragtime than anything else.

Even though Handy's music was not purely blues based, it was transformed into down-home blues by those who interpreted his songs. Most important, Handy's music brought the blues into the limelight during a time when America's musical identity was changing. By the 1920s, musicians of all races were performing and recording the blues. The blues could be heard on concert stages and on 78 rpm recordings by record labels such as Victor, Okeh, the American Record Corporation, and Paramount. The blues was developed by men in the American South. However, it was best promoted by women during the teens and twenties. Blues singers such as Mamie Smith, Gertrude "Ma" Rainey, Bessie Smith, Alberta Hunter, Ethel Waters, and Victoria Spivey helped bring the blues into the forefront of the American musical consciousness.

Styles of Blues

There are many styles of blues, and they are best understood through regionalism. As stated earlier, the blues was born in the rural South, but it was quickly transformed into an urban musical style. Cities such as Chicago, Detroit, Memphis, St. Louis, Kansas City, Dallas, Austin, Houston, Louisville, Los Angeles, New York City, and New Orleans all contributed to the development of the blues.

After World War I and World War II, black musicians from the Delta and Memphis moved to northern cities such as Detroit and Chicago. This was called the "Great Migration." Often this migration meant travel along Highway 51, which is a 1,286 mile stretch of road that connects La Place, Louisiana, to Hurley, Wisconsin. When Delta musicians arrived in Chicago, they began using amplifiers and soon the Chicago style was born. This sound was heavier and more plodding; even though it was still based around Delta techniques such as call and response (see Chapter 10).

In the mid-1940s, another migration occurred out of Texas. Blues musicians by the dozens left the Lone Star State to play on the West Coast. Most of these players landed in Los Angeles, though further migrations often took players to Berkeley and San Francisco. Significant Texas-born pianists who ventured westward include Little Willie Littlefield and Floyd Dixon. Soon, the so-called Texas style of blues merged into West Coast blues. This style was more smooth-toned and jazzy, and it contributed to the development of the black crooner tradition in the United States.

Other major styles of blues emerged in American cities, as you will read about in Chapter 11. Early on, Beale Street in Memphis became a melting pot for blues. In 1977, this street was declared the Home of the Blues by the U.S. Congress. New Orleans is a veritable "who's who" in piano blues, spawning such pianists as Jelly Roll Morton, Professor Longhair, Dr. John, and Harry Connick Jr. St. Louis was idealized in the eponymous "St. Louis Blues" by composer W. C. Handy. It was also home to the barrelhouse pianist Roosevelt Sykes and to the clever, Depression-era self-promoter Peetie Wheatstraw.

FACT

Barrelhouse piano was common in the rowdy drinking establishments of the South. It featured heavy, percussive, left-hand activity and was designed to make people dance. Barrelhouse—named after whiskey bars that poured directly from the cask—was the precursor to boogie-woogie.

In the ballrooms and saloons of Kansas City, swing was fashioned by pianists and bandleaders Jay McShann and Count Basie. Elsewhere, New York City was home to a chic, uptown style of jazz that drew heavily on the blues. This was probably best illustrated in the big band music of Duke Ellington and in the virtuosic stride styles of Fats Waller, Willie "The Lion" Smith, and James P. Johnson. Later in the book, you will read more about all these musicians and get the chance to play some of the licks and techniques that they employed in their music.

History of Rock

Rock-n-roll gained popularity in the early to mid 1950s due, in large part, to the development of the electric guitar, jukeboxes, television, and the 45 rpm record. Key figures such as Alan Freed, Sam Phillips, Jerry Leiber, Mike

Stoller, and others took advantage of this technology, captivating musicians and audiences alike with this new sound.

Sam Phillips's record label, Sun Records, had a major impact on the rise of rock-n-roll by signing Elvis Presley and assembling what would later be known as the Million Dollar Quartet, featuring Jerry Lee Lewis, Carl Perkins, Johnny Cash, and Presley himself. In 1954, Presley's "That's Alright Mama" scored well with audiences and 1956's "Heartbreak Hotel" became a number-one hit. Presley would become one of rock's most celebrated entertainers. He was eventually dubbed "the King of Rock-n-Roll."

In the 1950s, Fats Domino, Little Richard, and Jerry Lee Lewis quickly became the kings of rock piano. These stylists were all influenced by boogie-woogie and earlier piano blues traditions. However, they all had different musical upbringings, which accounts for their signature sounds. For example, Fats Domino was influenced by stride stylists and Dixieland jazz, Little Richard was enamored of gospel, and Jerry Lee Lewis drew heavily from country and western. Fats Domino was also fun-loving on stage. Little Richard and Jerry Lee Lewis were animated, even raucous, performers.

At its heart, rock-n-roll is a combination of rhythm and blues (black culture) and country and folk music (white culture). Rock grew out of the "race records" of three key blues styles: Delta blues, Chicago blues, and jump blues. It also combined elements from 1930s and 1940s country and folk music.

In 1964, the Beatles would land on American shores and leave an indelible mark on the collective consciousness of popular culture. Their influence is still powerful today. Even Elvis Presley's contributions would be overshadowed by the Fab Four. In the early days, the Beatles were inspired by 1950s rock-n-roll, specifically by the work of Chuck Berry, Eddie Cochran, Carl Perkins, Little Richard, the Everly Brothers, and Presley himself.

The Beatles would eventually dominate the 1960s with revolutionary albums such as *Revolver*, *Sgt. Pepper's Lonely Hearts Club Band*, *The White Album*, and *Abbey Road*. Even though they continued to find insight in the works of Bob Dylan and the Beach Boys, it was the Beatles who were clearly influencing others. Without a doubt, Beatlemania changed the course of pop history and the Fab Four have become something of an institution.

Technological Advancements

By the late 1960s, advances in synthesizer technology changed the role of piano players and organists who quickly embraced new electronic possibilities. Players such as Rick Wakeman (Yes) and Keith Emerson (Emerson, Lake, and Palmer) used analog Moog synthesizers quite effectively in their work. By the early 1980s, bands such as Rush, the Police, and U2 began using Moog Taurus bass pedal synthesizers to fatten up their sound. Around this time, most major pop acts also began experimenting with digital sampling synthesizers; the most popular were the Fairlight and the Synclavier.

In the last quarter of the twentieth century, keyboards featured prominently in the work of Stevie Wonder, Genesis, Peter Gabriel, Pink Floyd, the Talking Heads, the Cars, Roxy Music, Depeche Mode, Duran Duran, the Cure, Nine Inch Nails, and many, many others. However, no other group epitomizes the technological age quite like the German ensemble Kraftwerk, which you will read about in Chapter 14.

QUESTION?

What is Kraftwerk?
This ensemble's reclusive, even secretive lives have always been a part of their allure. Kraftwerk is led by Florian Schneider-Esleben and Ralf Hütter from Düsseldorf, Germany. Since 1970, this group has paved the way for DJ mix-masters, soundscape artists, remix pioneers, and more.

By the 1990s, advances in sampling technology meant the widespread use of digital pianos, which could simulate the sound of an acoustic piano with great accuracy. Today, many pianists use only keyboards. Even old blues players can be seen playing on hot new digital pianos. You will read all about analog and digital synthesizers, sampling, digital pianos, and more in Chapter 16.

Styles of Rock

There are many styles of rock, and the list keeps growing as new hybrids are developed. Almost since its inception, rock-n-roll has mutated into offshoots or subgenres. It's hard to even keep up with the new styles that emerge (and fade away) with each passing decade. Some of these movements are regional and never really get off the ground. Others are retro and, therefore, disappear after a new fad comes along.

Some noteworthy substyles of rock include rockabilly, folk rock, country rock, Latin rock, Christian rock, southern rock, psychedelic rock, stoner rock, progressive rock, hard rock, heavy metal, punk rock, new wave, garage rock, grunge, alternative rock, death metal, and indie rock. Many would argue that rock also gave birth to techno, electronica, rap, and hip-hop.

In this book, you will learn about the following major movements in rock:

- R&B and early rock-n-roll (1950s)
- The British invasion and psychedelic rock (1960s)
- Progressive and hard rock (1970s)
- Funk and soul (1970s)
- The second British invasion, new wave, and synth pop (1980s)
- Contemporary hybrids (1990s and beyond)

Since this book revolves around the piano, you will also learn about pop pianists/songwriters such as Elton John, Billy Joel, Randy Newman, and to a lesser extent newer faces like Tori Amos, Ben Folds, Rufus Wainwright, and others. Grouped together you could call this "piano rock" or "piano pop." Differentiating between those terms is something to explore as well and distinctions will be made about the sometimes hazy discrepancy between pop and rock in Chapter 12.

Rock virtually ruled the popular music roost until rap and hip-hop came along and topped it in CD sales in the 1990s. However, rock continues to have an enormous impact on popular culture. More and more, it is being re-energized and reorganized by musicians who are combining rap and hip-hop with rock's thunderous grooves and sonic presence. Rock instruments such as electric guitars, drum sets, and bass guitars are also being incorporated more and more into modern R&B settings (as opposed to drum machines and other computerized filler). This suggests rock's assertiveness in an era when computer technology could put any instrumentalist out of work.

In 1999, file sharing became popular due to advancements in Internet technology and a company called Napster. To this day, file sharing, CD burning, and illegal downloads continue to be hot topics in the record industry. Arguments for and against music sharing are likely to continue as intellectual property rights are disputed online and in courtrooms worldwide.

One thing's for sure: It's safe to say that keyboards are here to stay. Artists of all genres and subgenres readily use keyboards and synthesizers in both the studio and on the stage. Moreover, blues and rock piano licks from earlier generations are being rediscovered as up-and-coming artists root their tunes in older, more traditional styles.

Chapter 2

An Overview of the Piano

This chapter is broken down into two sections. First, you will learn about keyboard layout together with basic music theory. Second, you will learn about posture and proper hand and finger positioning. This chapter should only serve as a quick tutorial. If you are brand-new to this instrument, you may want to seek additional information from a qualified instructor. Everything stated here applies to both the piano and the electric keyboard.

Keyboard Layout

The piano keyboard is well laid out, with notes repeating themselves every twelve keys. When a key is pressed, a hammer strikes a series of strings and a pitch sounds. The pitches move from low to high, left to right. In other words, when you sit at the piano, the lowest pitch will be to your left and the highest pitch will be to your right. If you're sitting at your piano now, strike the highest and lowest keys. You will hear a distinct difference between them. Modern pianos and most professional digital pianos contain eighty-eight keys.

FACT

Pitch is the frequency of a note, which is measured in cycles per second. In the modern era, concert A—located a major sixth above middle C—is set at 440 Hertz (Hz). This is the standard pitch that orchestras use to tune their instruments. In Western music, equal pitch divisions occur within the so-called twelve-tone temperament system.

The keys on a piano are white and black, and they each have letter names. The white keys are A, B, C, D, E, F, and G. Collectively, these notes are called "naturals." After G, the lettering begins again with A. This A to G sequence occurs seven full times on an eighty-eight-key piano. After the seven times, three additional notes remain: A, B, and C.

Each note on the keyboard is also given a numerical name. These numbers correspond to the placement of the note on the piano. The numbering system begins with zero. The first or lowest note on the keyboard is A0. The top note is C8, since it is the eighth C to appear on the keyboard. The twenty-fourth note up from the bottom, when counting only white keys, is middle C. This is called C4, since it is the fourth C on the keyboard. In other words, three Cs precede middle C as you travel from left to right up the keyboard.

Accidentals

An accidental is any pitch that is not found in the key signature (see Chapter 4). The black keys on the piano are usually referred to as accidentals but white keys can also be called accidentals given certain musical contexts. As you will learn in Chapter 4, some keys are written with sharps ♯. Others are written with flats ♭. Either way, both naturals and accidentals are enharmonic. This simply means that all notes have two note names. For example, C-sharp can also be called D-flat. B-flat can also be called A-sharp. B-natural can also be called C-flat, F can also be called E sharp, and so on.

Like notes, key signatures are also enharmonic. For example, the key of F-sharp can also be called G-flat, A-flat can be called G-sharp, and so on. Thankfully, musical convention saves you from the dreaded task of reading music in odd keys such as G-sharp. This key would contain an F-double sharp (G) and a B-sharp (C).

Only context can help you choose the correct enharmonic note name. Usually, the key signature dictates the enharmonic spelling of a note. Moreover, chord functions may also determine the spelling of an accidental or altered tone.

Visualizing the Keyboard

Keyboard layout can be visualized in two distinct groups or clusters. The first group consists of C, C-sharp (also called D-flat), D, D-sharp (also called E-flat), and E. Visually, this layout contains three white keys and two black keys: five keys total. This configuration appears on an eighty-eight-key piano seven full times. It is shown in **FIGURE 2-1**.

The next group of notes includes F, F-sharp (also called G-flat), G, G-sharp (also called A-flat), A, A-sharp (also called B-flat), and B: seven keys total. As does the previous note group, this configuration appears on an eighty-eight-key keyboard seven full times. It is shown in **FIGURE 2-2**.

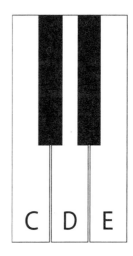

FIGURE 2-1: C–E Keyboard Layout

FIGURE 2-2: F–B
Keyboard Layout

When you put these two groups together, you have twelve keys total (that's five plus seven). If you include one more note on the top—a C—the cycle will be complete. That same C also signals the beginning of a new cycle. A full-note cycle from C to C is indicated in **FIGURE 2-3**. Later, you will call this cycle an octave.

Whole- and Half-Step Intervals

An interval is the distance between two notes. In Western music, intervals are measured in steps. A melodic, or linear, interval refers to two notes that are played one at a time. A harmonic, or vertical, interval refers to two notes that are played simultaneously. When two notes are played together they create a chord called a dyad. Steps are broken down into (1) whole steps (also called whole tones) and (2) half steps (also called semitones). Whole steps are a combination of two half steps. Half steps are chromatic movements on the keyboard. When you count half steps, you will count all the consecutive white and black keys from one note (*x*) to another note (*y*). Never skip notes when counting half steps. Consider the interval between C and D. If you

FIGURE 2-3: C–C
Keyboard Layout

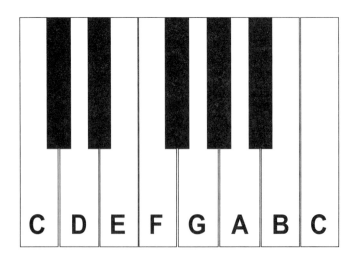

count up the keyboard chromatically, you will notice that there are two half steps between C and D. They are C to C-sharp and C-sharp to D.

Together, they add up to one whole step. Again, one whole step equals two half steps. Try another example. Look at C on the piano. Pretend that C is your bottom note or home base. Now count up seven half steps to G. The half steps are as follows:

1. C to C-sharp
2. C-sharp to D
3. D to D-sharp
4. D-sharp to E
5. E to F
6. F to F-sharp
7. F-sharp to G

Remember, when you count half steps, you are traveling chromatically up or down the keyboard.

QUESTION?

What's a simple way to tell the difference between whole and half steps on the piano?

Compare two adjacent white keys. If there's a black key between them, the interval is a whole step. For example, G and A are divided by a B-flat (or A-sharp). The adjacent keys E and F, and B and C have no black keys between them. Therefore, they are half steps.

Understanding Octaves

As hinted at earlier, octaves are intervals that span twelve half steps. When playing octaves, the bottom note will bear the same letter name as the top note (for example, A–A, B–B, C–C). Choose a note and play it on the piano. Now count twelve half steps higher or lower. If you count correctly, the note you end on will be one octave higher or lower than the original note you played. Take the note E as an example. Now count in ascending half steps:

1. F
2. F-sharp
3. G
4. G-sharp
5. A
6. A-sharp
7. B
8. C
9. C-sharp
10. D
11. D-sharp
12. E (perfect octave)

Octaves have a 2:1 ratio. For example, concert A is standardized at 440 Hz. The A above this frequency is 880 Hz, which is exactly double the frequency of concert A. The A below concert A is 220 Hz, which is exactly one-half the frequency of concert A.

Scale Degrees

As you learned earlier in the chapter, it's important to know how to count intervals in half steps. However, intervals are more often counted in scale degrees. You will learn more about scale degrees in Chapter 4. For now, accept on faith that the key of C major uses all white notes. The following list shows you how to count scalar (diatonic) intervals. These intervals are called either "major" or "perfect."

- C to C (no movement) is a perfect unison.
- C to D is a major second.
- C to E is a major third.
- C to F is a perfect fourth.
- C to G is a perfect fifth.
- C to A is a major sixth.
- C to B is a major seventh.
- C to C (twelve half steps higher) is a perfect octave.

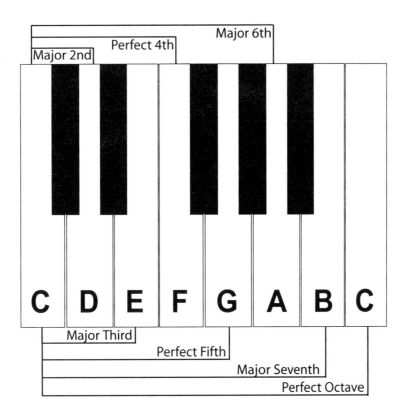

FIGURE 2-4:

Diatonic Intervals

These same diatonic intervals are shown in **FIGURE 2-4**.

Once you add accidentals, interval counting becomes more complex. What's more, these intervals can now be called a variety of names depending on the musical context. Here is a list of intervals that uses C as the bottom note and an accidental as the top note. The intervals with an asterisk next to them are used the most in music writing; the others are more or less academic.

- C to C-sharp is an augmented unison.
- C to D-flat is a minor second*.
- C to D-sharp is an augmented second.
- C to E-flat is a minor third*.
- C to E-sharp (enharmonically this is an F) is an augmented third.
- C to F-flat (enharmonically this is an E) is a diminished fourth.
- C to F-sharp is an augmented fourth (also called a tri-tone)*.

- C to G-flat is a diminished fifth (also called a tri-tone)*.
- C to G-sharp is an augmented fifth.
- C to A-flat is a minor sixth*.
- C to A-sharp is an augmented sixth.
- C to B-flat is a minor seventh*.
- C to C-flat is a diminished octave.

In this book, the interval between C and B-flat will often be referred to as a dominant seventh because of its relationship to a dominant seventh chord in blues music. Technically, however, this interval is a minor seventh because the seventh scale degree is flatted.

Once you pass the octave mark, other important intervals arise, such as ninths, tenths, elevenths, and thirteenths. In this book, you will also see sharp nines and flat nines, sharp elevens, and flatted thirteenths.

In the following chapters, the terms *scale degree*, *major*, *minor*, *augmented*, and *diminished* will be defined for you. For now, just make sure you understand whole and half steps.

Sitting at the Piano or Keyboard

Although some pianists sit in an unorthodox position at the piano, you should focus on good posture. But what is a proper sitting position? This is a debatable subject and classical composers Carl Philipp Emanuel Bach, Muzio Clementi, Johann Nepomuk Hummel, Carl Czerny, and others have all weighed in on this topic through essays and other writings. As your playing develops, you should continue to refine your sitting position. For now, try the approach outlined here. This sitting position will help to reduce strain in the lumbar region of the back. It will also promote relaxation in the upper and lower extremities.

First, set the piano bench in front of the piano keys. Make sure you place it in the middle of the keys. If it is off to one side, you will be stretching to reach notes. Next, sit down in the middle of the piano bench. Again, if you sit off to one side, your playing will suffer. Make sure the bench isn't too close to the keyboard. You should be able to slide easily in between the keyboard and the bench to sit down. Once you're seated, place your right foot on the sustain pedal. Does it feel comfortable? If the bench is properly positioned, your heel will sit on the floor and your leg will bend at a slightly obtuse angle. If the bench is too close to the pedals, your heel may cock upward. The proper positioning for your left leg should be around 90 degrees (a right angle).

Be very careful how you sit on the piano bench. You should sit on the edge of the bench. This means that your upper thighs should not be touching the bench. Do not lounge on the piano bench. Never cross your legs, sit sidesaddle, or inch toward the corners of the bench as you play.

Once you're seated, sit up straight. Make sure your upper body is erect. Your spine should not be curved, and your shoulders should not be rolled inward. Think about how military personnel stand when they are at attention. Once you're sitting upright, tilt your upper body slightly toward the keyboard. When you are seated properly you should feel comfortable and secure, not unbalanced and awkward.

Be careful not to sit with your muscles clenched. You never want to feel stiff. Your upper body should sway ever so slightly as you create musical phrases. In other words, in order to play the piano with expression and feeling, you will need to shift your weight from time to time. This may mean leaning in to play an accent or louder passage or pulling back to play a pianissimo (soft) line. However, never slide your buttocks on the piano bench. Always remain firmly planted on the bench even when you are playing in the highest and lowest registers of the keyboard. If the piano bench cannot adjust to your body size, feel free to use mats or carpet samples to add bench height. Don't sit on books; they can be wobbly and uncomfortable, especially if you're playing for long periods.

Hand and Finger Placement

Proper hand and finger placement on the keyboard is essential. Like your right leg position, your elbows should be bent at an obtuse angle. Moreover, always keep your forearms parallel to the floor and adjust the bench so that you're not unconsciously lifting your shoulders. Once again, don't hesitate to use mats or carpet samples to add height.

Your wrists should be in a slightly flexed position. The keys should be right under your fingertips when you flex your wrists slightly upward. Be careful not to flex your wrists upward in an extreme position. Similarly, do not allow your wrists to dip or extend downward so that your fingers point upward. Also, never tense or lock your wrists. Your fingers, wrists, arms, and shoulders should always feel relaxed and free of any tension.

Finger position is also critical. Always play with your fingertips. The best way to learn basic finger position is to pretend that you are holding a ball. When you do this, your hand will naturally cup, allowing you to press down on the keys with the tips of your fingers. If you extend your fingers outward, so that they are straight, you will give yourself a severe musical handicap and you won't be able to maneuver around the keyboard. When you play, you should see your knuckles. Your hand should never be flat.

One of the best ways to learn proper finger technique is to watch classical pianists perform. Classical players maintain very high technical standards, and they are extremely efficient and graceful in their movements. When observing them, their fingers will seem to travel effortlessly up and down the keyboard and they always play on their fingertips.

The good news is that when you place your hand on the keyboard, your fingers will probably automatically form a cup shape. Rarely is finger positioning a lasting problem for students. When playing the black keys, your fingers may extend a little farther to reach these notes. This is okay especially if you have small hands.

It's also important to know where to press down on the piano keys. When playing white keys, the index and middle fingers will press down slightly above the middle of the fat part of the piano key. The ring finger should press down in the middle of the key and the pinky finger should press down slightly below the middle of the key. Because of the placement of the thumb on the hand, this digit presses down on the edge of the keys. When playing chords or melodies with a lot of black keys, you should shift your basic hand position to the black notes. In this case, follow the finger position in the exact same fashion: The index and middle fingers will press down in the middle of the key, the ring finger will press down in the middle of the key, the pinky finger will press down slightly below the middle of the key, and the thumb will press down on the edge of the key. When in this position, you will play the white keys with your fingertips on the thinner part of the key. You still need to maintain a cupped shape in your hand. **FIGURE 2-5** shows proper posture and arm, hand, and finger position at the piano.

Fingering in the Right and Left Hands

Fingering is one of the most important aspects of piano playing. Without careful and thoughtful fingering, you will fumble and play sloppily. Since this is not a beginner method book, it is assumed that you know something about fingering on the piano. Therefore, fingering is not indicated in each and every

FIGURE 2-5:
Correct Posture:
Arm, Hand, and
Finger Position on
the Piano

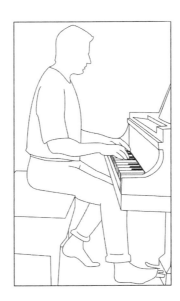

exercise. On particularly "snaky" musical exercises, fingering will be included. Also, basic fingering for most scales and arpeggios will also be included.

However, many of the exercises and study pieces found later in the book can be interpreted in a number of ways. There is not always one way to finger each phrase or musical passage. Often, it comes down to personal preference, which is based on your hand size and your skill level. Recognizing this, you will need to map out your own fingering on select musical examples. Take the time to do this. Don't leave fingering to chance unless you are a really adept pianist. For most intermediate-level players, it's important to consider fingering options before attempting to play a piece of music.

If you're self-taught, you might not know the fingering system used in musical notation. On both hands, the thumbs are called finger one, the index fingers are called finger two, the middle fingers are called finger three, the ring fingers are called finger four, and the pinky fingers are called finger five. See **FIGURE 2-6**.

Each finger has its strengths and weaknesses. Since the thumb is situated on the side of the hand, it must cross under the fingers to maneuver up the keyboard. This can be tricky and this movement requires practice. The index (pointer) fingers and middle fingers are the strongest. The ring fingers are least coordinated, and the pinky fingers are usually the weakest. Whether you play rock, blues, or any other style of music, it's important to practice technical exercises to develop strength and stamina in all of your fingers.

FIGURE 2-6:
Fingering Chart

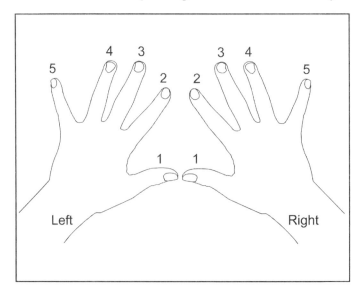

Chapter 3
Notation as a Tool

Musicians use notation to study music and to communicate musical ideas. In this chapter, you will learn the nuts and bolts of musical notation. Included in this tutorial will be information on notes, rests, clefs, pitches, time signatures, and much more. You will find that having the ability to read music makes life as a musician a lot easier and a lot more rewarding. Notation will help you unlock the elements of rock and blues.

Notation Overview

Why should you learn how to read music? For the same reason you learn how to read words. If you're musically literate, your chances of survival in the world of music greatly improve. By learning to read music, you will be able to visualize music better and, therefore, be able to conceive of music more clearly. Musical literacy will expand your musical vocabulary, augment your communication skills, and allow you to better store musical thoughts.

ALERT!

Playing solely by ear can be limiting, especially when you are trying to learn from a book. The CD in the back of this guide is a great supplement, but it cannot replace the notation found in each chapter. Therefore, in order to get the most out of this text, make sure you learn how to read music.

All music can be divided into two parts: sound and silence. Notes represent the sounds a musician makes. Rests indicate silence. Both are written on a staff. A staff is a set of five parallel lines on which a composer writes notes, rests, and other musical symbols. See **FIGURE 3-1**.

The lines and spaces on a staff represent pitch varieties; a clef is used to name each line and space. The most common clefs are treble or G clef and bass or F clef, although alto and tenor clefs also exist. As a pianist, you will use only the treble and bass clefs.

Range, Treble, and Bass Clefs

With the exception of the harp and other keyboard instruments, no other instrument uses two clefs at once. As a pianist, you are expected to play and read music from two clefs for one very important reason: range. By looking at **FIGURE 2-3**, which shows the keyboard layout, you will see that the range of the piano is more than eight octaves. No single clef can accommodate such a span, hence the use of both treble and bass.

The octave range found on a piano is very rare among instruments. For example, the average tenor voice can only sing a little over two and one-half octaves (B2–G4). The trumpet can only play about three and one-half octaves (F3-sharp–F6-sharp). But this is the beauty of the piano. It can create a full symphony of sound.

FIGURE 3-1: A
Blank Staff

FIGURE 3-2:
Treble Clef

You will need to memorize the look of both the treble or G clef and the bass or F clef in order to read music. **FIGURE 3-2** shows the treble clef. **FIGURE 3-3** shows the bass clef.

The two clefs look very different from each other, so it should be easy to distinguish between them when reading music. Also,

FIGURE 3-3:
Bass Clef

the treble clef will always appear above or on top of the bass clef. If you remember this small detail, you will never confuse the clefs.

Pitches and Clefs

In **FIGURE 3-4**, you see the two staves used for piano music. Together, they form one super-sized staff called the grand staff.

Notes are written on both the lines and the spaces of each staff. In order to name the pitches, a clef is used; the clef defines or delineates each line and space. The best way to understand this is through example. The first space from the bottom in the treble clef is F. The first space from the bottom

FIGURE 3-4:
The Grand
Staff

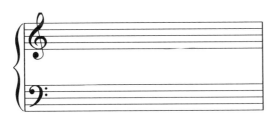

FIGURE 3-5:
Comparing Clefs

in the bass clef is A. The spaces look the same, but they represent different notes (and even different octaves). This is illustrated in **FIGURE 3-5**.

In the following figures, a generic note head will signify pitch. Later in the chapter, you will learn about note names and rhythms. **FIGURE 3-6** shows you all of the lines and spaces for each clef. Use a mnemonic device to help you remember the lines and spaces. In **FIGURE 3-6**, the word FACE represents the spaces on the treble clef. Read it from the bottom up.

FIGURE 3-6: F A C E on the Treble Clef

FIGURE 3-7: Every Good Boy Does Fine on the Treble Clef

To remember the lines on the treble clef, think of EGBDF as an acronym for Every Good Boy Does Fine. Again, read from the bottom up. See **FIGURE 3-7**.

Follow the same procedure for the bass clef. To remember the spaces, use the mnemonic device 'All Cows Eat Grass'. See **FIGURE 3-8**.

For the lines on the bass clef, use the phrase Good Boys Do Fine Always. See **FIGURE 3-9**.

FIGURE 3-8: All Cows Eat Grass on the Bass Clef

FIGURE 3-9: Good Boys Do Fine Always on the Bass Clef

Ledger Lines and Octaves

Ledger lines are tiny, horizontal lines that appear above or below the staff. Since the staff only captures nine intervals, ledger lines are needed to document those notes that exist in the piano's upper and lower registers. When it

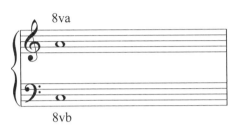

FIGURE 3-10:
8va and 8vb

is necessary to write extremely low or high notes, the terms *8va* or *8vb* are written above or below the notes, respectively. See **FIGURE 3-10**. For example, 8va tells the pianist that he or she must play (or transpose) the music exactly one octave above what is

written, while 8vb tells the pianist to play the music exactly one octave lower than written. These terms help the pianist read with greater ease.

Ledger lines are important, especially the ones used to represent middle C. In **FIGURE 2-3**, the keyboard layout, you learned where middle C is situated on the piano. Now, let's look at middle C on the treble and bass clefs. (See **FIGURES 3-11** and **3-12**). Notice that middle C hangs below the staff in the treble clef and above the staff in the bass clef.

FIGURE 3-11: Middle C on the Treble Clef

FIGURE 3-12: Middle C on the Bass Clef

We can also use ledger lines for higher or lower pitches. **FIGURE 3-13** shows the grand staff with three ledger lines above and three ledger lines

FIGURE 3-13:
Extended
Ledger Lines

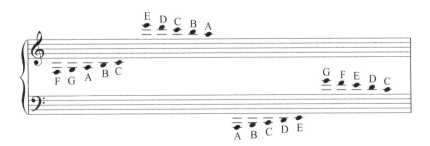

below each staff. If you wish to write notes lower or higher than this, it is better to use 8va or 8vb.

Note Names and Rhythm

Along with melody and harmony, rhythm is one of the most important elements in music. A note is made up of a note head and a note stem. The only exception to this is a whole note, which does not contain a stem. A note head is seen either as an empty circle (whole or half notes) or as a black dot (all other notes). A note stem is a vertical line that is attached to the note head. If you see a single stem attached to a solid black note head you are looking at a quarter note. If that note head is empty or hollow, you are looking at a half note. Sometimes notes are connected or barred together by a single horizontal line; this notation is used to indicate eighth notes. You might also see a double horizontal line; this is used to indicate sixteenth notes. Still other notes have a wavy line that curves down the stem; this is called a flag. A single flag is used to signify one eighth note. A double flag is used to signify one sixteenth note. See **FIGURE 3-14**.

FIGURE 3-14:
Notes Barred
Together

whole   half   quarter   eighth   barred eighths   sixteenth   barred sixteenths

Notice that individual eighth notes look exactly the same as quarter notes but with a flag attached. The individual sixteenth note also looks like the quarter note but with two flags attached.

ALERT!

The British use different names for notes. They call a whole note a semibreve, a half note a minim, a quarter note a crochet, an eighth note a quaver, and a sixteenth note a semiquaver. Don't be confused by this, and unless you live in the United Kingdom, don't use these terms.

Table of Notes

Musical notation is based on mathematics. Notation follows the same rules as fractions. **FIGURE 3-15** shows the division of notes.

1:2 Ratio

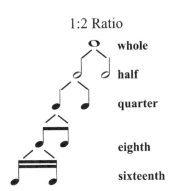

FIGURE 3-15: Divisional Relationship of Notes

As you can see, notes divide into two equal parts. A whole note divides into two half notes, a half note divides into two quarter notes, a quarter note divides into two eighth notes, and an eighth note divides into two sixteenth notes. When making these divisions, a 1:2 ratio occurs between the whole and half note, the half and quarter note, the quarter and eighth note, and the eighth and sixteenth note. The pie charts in **FIGURES 3-16** through **3-19** should help make this clearer.

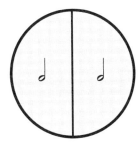

FIGURE 3-16: Divisional Foundation of Notes—Half Notes

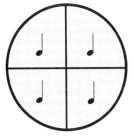

FIGURE 3-17: Divisional Foundation of Notes—Quarter Notes

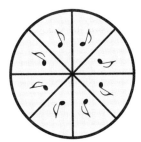

FIGURE 3-18: Divisional Foundation of Notes—Eighth Notes

FIGURE 3-19: Divisional Foundation of Notes—Sixteenth Notes

You can see that two half notes equal the whole pie, four quarter notes equal the whole pie, eight eighth notes equal the whole pie, and sixteen sixteenth notes equal the whole pie. This is the mathematical backbone of notation.

Rests

Rests function in exactly the same way as notes but with one key difference. Whereas a note signifies sound, a rest equals silence. A rest does not mean to pause. The music continues whether you're resting or not or whether there is sound or not. Think of a rest as a silent note.

FIGURE 3-20:
Divisional
Relationship of
Rests

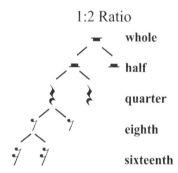

1:2 Ratio

whole

half

quarter

eighth

sixteenth

When resting, always follow the music the same as if you were playing. Every note has a corresponding rest and rests have the same relationship to one another as notes do. **FIGURE 3-20** shows each type of rest as it is divided from whole to sixteenth.

Time Signatures

Now that you have been exposed to notes and rests, you must piece them together to make rhythmical sentences. To accomplish this, you must first learn about time signatures.

There are many time signatures used in music. For example, 3/4 is used for waltzes, and 2/2 and 6/8 are typically used by marching bands. Since most rock and blues music uses 4/4, this book will focus almost exclusively on this time signature.

Dissecting 4/4

All time signatures contain a top number and a bottom number. These numbers tell the musician two important things: (1) how many beats there are in a measure, and (2) what note value equals one beat.

This definition requires an understanding of additional jargon; namely, what a measure and a beat are. Most music is played in time; it has a pulse that once started continues until the composition reaches its end. This pulse is called the beat.

Notes and rests are segmented into smaller compartments of time. These boxes of time are called measures or bars. Notes and rests are contained within measures, and bar lines are used to mark each measure's borders. As you will see in **FIGURE 3-21**, bar lines are simple vertical lines used to separate measures.

FIGURE 3-21:
Grand Staff
with Bar Line

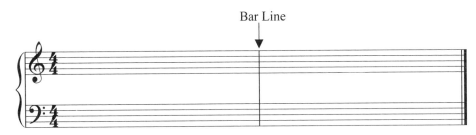
Bar Line

Think of 4/4 time as a fraction, even though technically it is not. You will notice in the examples found later in the book that there is no line dividing the two number fours. The fours merely sit on top of each other.

However, for educational purposes, temporarily accept 4/4 as a fraction. All fractions have a top number called a numerator and a bottom number called a denominator. The numerator will tell you how many beats you have in a measure. The denominator will tell you what note value equals one beat. In order to do this, though, you must first replace the numerator with a one.

FACT

Another name for 4/4 is common time. If you turn the radio on and flip through the stations, you will hear 4/4 used on most songs. No other time signature is used so often in music. Part of the reason for this is the symmetrical nature of 4/4: 2+2 is easy to dance to.

Since there is a four in the numerator, there are four beats in each measure. If you temporarily take away the top four and place a one in the numerator, you are left with one-fourth or a quarter. This tells you that the quarter note equals the beat. So in 4/4, you have four beats in a measure and the quarter note represents each beat.

Quarter and Eighth Notes

Quarter notes function as the pulse or beat in most of the music you will play. Ninety-eight percent of the music you will hear uses the quarter note as its heartbeat. When you place four quarter notes into a measure of 4/4, it is counted like **FIGURE 3-22**.

FIGURE 3-22:
Four Quarter
Notes

Each quarter note represents a downbeat. In 4/4, downbeats equal the numbers one, two, three, and four. If you divide quarter notes into eighth notes, you will have eight of them per measure. It looks like **FIGURE 3-23**.

FIGURE 3-23 divided the beat into two parts. It should be counted "1-and, 2-and, 3-and, 4-and." *Ands* are called upbeats. Upbeats represent the second half of a beat. A plus sign is used in this figure, and throughout the book to signify an upbeat or "and."

FIGURE 3-23:
One Measure of
Eighth Notes

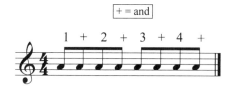

Straight Eighths Versus Swing Eighths

In this book, you will play eighth notes two different ways. You will play them "straight," and you will play them "swing." When you play them straight, you will play them exactly as described earlier. However, when you play them with a swing feel, you will play them as triplets. To better understand this, look at **FIGURE 3-24**. This figure shows you one measure of triplets. Bear in mind that these are not yet "swing" eighth notes, but rather, their rhythmical underpinning.

Straight eighth notes are duple, meaning they divide into two equal parts. As you can see in **FIGURE 3-25**, triplets divide into three equal parts (triple). The final step in creating swing eighths is to take out the middle triplet and add a rest. When you take this note out, the swing eighths appear.

Look at **FIGURE 3-26**, and tap the eighth notes using the rhythm you learned in **FIGURE 3-25**. When you do this, you will be interpreting straight eighths as swing eighths. Why do you do this? Since triplets are hard to read, copyists have long

used  to mean . This is simply shorthand. In this book, if nothing is indicated in the music telling you to interpret eighths as triplets, *always* read them straight.

Three Triplets = One Beat

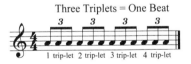

FIGURE 3-24: Triplets

Also written using a quarter - eighth triplet pattern as seen below . . .

FIGURE 3-25: Swing Eighths Written as Triplets

Keeping Time and Counting Aloud

One of the most important facets of music is timekeeping. Without a good internal clock, you will have limited ability to play with other musicians. As previously stated, music exists in time and space. Time refers to the pulse of the music, while space refers to the rhythmical components—notes and rests—that exist within a time span.

FIGURE 3-26:
Swing Eighths

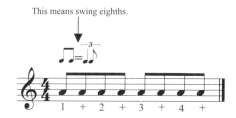

Most of the music you will play in this book exists inside a strict box of time. However, this is not true of all music. Classical, for example, is often played *rubato*, or without time. Rubato is also used by blues artists whose work revolves around storytelling or vocal narratives.

However, as a student of music, you should focus on timekeeping. If you don't, your understanding of rhythms will suffer. You will definitely sell yourself short if you practice out of time (rubato) or if you fail to count off before you play.

As previously stated, when you see four quarter notes, you should count the downbeats: 1, 2, 3, 4. Counting divisions and subdivisions is also helpful. For instance, you know that eighth notes are counted: 1-and, 2-and, 3-and, 4-and. Sixteenth notes are counted using the syllables: 1, e, and, ah / 2, e, and, ah / 3, e, and, ah / 4, e, and, ah. See **FIGURE 3-27**.

No matter what, you must always count off before you begin playing. This applies to both beginners and professionals. A tempo must always be established in order to play music. Counting off solidifies the tempo and helps to avoid musical train wrecks.

FIGURE 3-27:
Counting
Sixteenth Notes

Chapter 4

Keys, Scales, Pedaling, and Technique Building

In this chapter, you will learn more about music theory. More specifically, you will be introduced to keys and scales, the foundation of Western tonal music. Whether you play rock or blues, make sure you understand these concepts first. You really won't be able to play any of the styles in this book without this knowledge. Next, you'll find information on pedaling, and the chapter closes with exercises geared toward developing finger strength and control.

4

Key Signatures

There are fifteen keys used in Western tonal music. With the exception of C major and its counterpart A minor, each key is identified by a series of flats or sharps. Flats and sharps are written on the staff in a specific order; they are never combined. In a key signature, the set of sharps or flats is written after the clef but before the time signature. All notes written in the body of a piece of music defer to the key signature. For example, if the key signature indicates the presence of an F-sharp all Fs found in the composition will be sharp. If a songwriter does want the performer to play an F-natural, he or she will write a natural sign ♮ next to the note.

To the deft ear, each key bears a specific musical "color" or "personality." As a result, composers and songwriters alike sometimes have favorite keys. Key signatures have practical value, too. They are used to avoid writing lots of sharps or flats in the body of the music. Too many accidentals make a piece of music look overly complicated.

Additionally, key signatures identify a piece of music's home base, as it were. Most songs contain resolution or musical periods. A song's conclusion usually matches the key. For example, if you're in the key of C major, the song will probably end on a C major chord. Further, key signatures define the primary scale or mode of a song. In turn, this mode defines the specific chord names (not types) used. As music gets more and more complex, there are exceptions to these rules.

Each key signature denotes two keys: a major key and a relative minor key. The relative minor key uses the same set of pitches as its major counterpart. The minor key is defined by three scales that begin and end a minor third below (or a major sixth above) the relative major. The relative minor key also uses its own set of cadences (see Chapter 6).

FIGURE 4-1 shows you all the sharp keys. To identify sharp keys, look at the last sharp and then raise the pitch one half step. For example, the key

FIGURE 4-1:
Major and
Minor Sharp
Keys

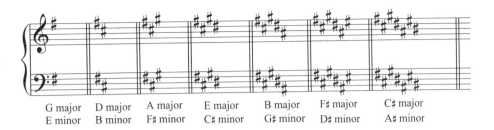

G major   D major   A major   E major   B major   F♯ major   C♯ major
E minor   B minor   F♯ minor   C♯ minor   G♯ minor   D♯ minor   A♯ minor

of A major has three sharps (F-sharp, C-sharp, and G-sharp). One half step above G-sharp is A.

FIGURE 4-2 shows you all the flat keys. To identify flat keys, look at the penultimate or second-to-last flat. That flat indicates the key. For example, the key of A-flat major has four flats (B-flat, E-flat, A-flat, and D-flat). The second-to-last flat is A-flat. Therefore, the key is A-flat. You will need to memorize the major and minor key signatures with one flat. They are F major and D minor, respectively.

FIGURE 4-2:
Major and
Minor Flat Keys

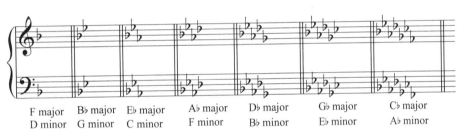

F major   B♭ major   E♭ major   A♭ major   D♭ major   G♭ major   C♭ major
D minor   G minor   C minor   F minor   B♭ minor   E♭ minor   A♭ minor

There are a number of mnemonic devices used by students to remember the order of the sharps and flats on the staff. One memory tool for remembering sharps is Fat Cows Get Dizzy After Eating Barley (F, C, G, D, A, E, B). A memory device for remembering the order of flats is BEAD Go Call Fred (B, E, A, D, G, C, F).

FACT

C major and A minor use all naturals (no sharps or flats) in their key signatures. Therefore, these key signatures have not been included in **FIGURES 4-1** and **4-2**. However, as you will learn later on, the A harmonic minor scale and the A melodic minor scale both use accidentals.

Major Scales

Scales, in Western tonal music, are derived from ancient Greek modes. A scale is really just a predetermined set of intervals. Scales are the building blocks of music, including rock and blues. The major scale, also called the Ionian mode, comprises the following intervals: whole, whole, half, whole, whole, whole, half. If you sit at the keyboard, choose a random starting note, and then use this intervallic formula, you will always play a major scale.

For example, the C major scale consists of the following notes: C, D, E, F, G, A, B, C. The interval between C and D is a whole step. The interval between D and E is a whole step. The interval between E and F is a half step. The interval between F and G is a whole step. The interval between G and A is a whole step. The interval between A and B is a whole step, and the interval between B and C is a half step.

As you read in Chapter 2, intervals are typically counted using scale degrees. The names of the seven scale degrees are outlined here:

1. First degree: tonic
2. Second degree: supertonic
3. Third degree: mediant
4. Fourth degree: subdominant
5. Fifth degree: dominant
6. Sixth degree: submediant
7. Seventh degree: subtonic (leading tone)

The ascending C major scale is shown in **FIGURE 4-3**. Whole steps, half steps, and scale degrees are also indicated.

FIGURE 4-3:
Ascending C
Major Scale

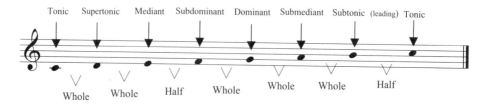

FIGURE 4-4 shows you the C major scale, plus all seven sharp keyed major scales. The scales are written for both hands in octaves. When you play this figure, be mindful of the key signatures. Remember, if a key contains sharps or flats, they must always be observed. Also, be sure to follow the fingering.

FIGURE 4-4: C Major and Sharp Key Major Scales

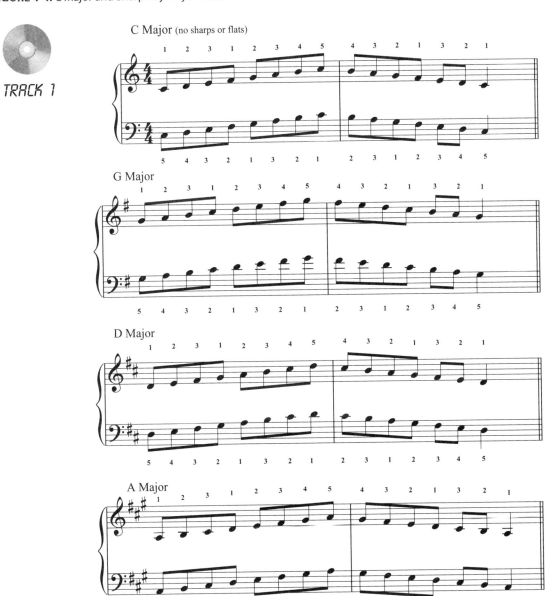

As you play, your hands should be in perfect sync. Strive to create smooth melodic lines.

FIGURE 4-4 (continued): C Major and Sharp Key Major Scales

FIGURE 4-5 shows you all of the flat key major scales. Don't forget about proper technique when playing scales. Make sure your hands remain cupped as if holding a ball. If necessary, see Chapter 2 for a review of this important hand and finger position.

FIGURE 4-5: Flat Key Major Scales

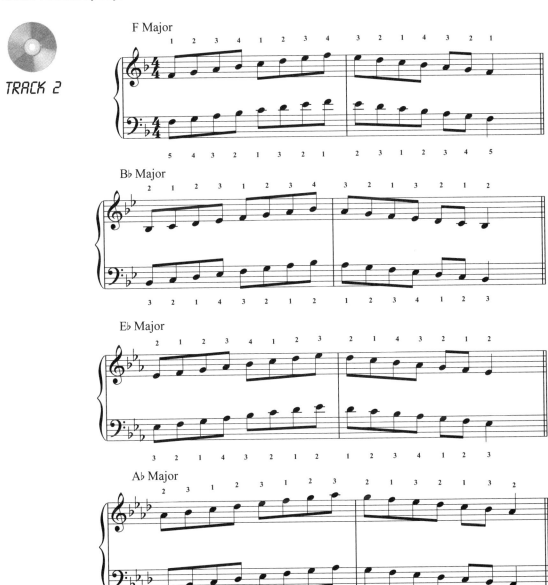

FIGURE 4-5 (continued): Flat Key Major Scales

Minor Scales

The minor scale, also called the Aeolian mode, is closely related to the major scale. As you learned earlier, major and minor scales are "relative" keys. The difference lies in the start and stop points and in the positioning of the scale degrees. For example, the note E in the key of C major is a major third. The note E in the key of A minor (the relative minor of C) is a perfect fifth.

Do not confuse relative minor/major with parallel minor/major. Parallel refers to two keys that have the same start point or tonic (e.g., C major and C minor). However, parallel major/minor keys are not related by key signature.

For instance, if you compare C major and C minor, you will notice that C major contains no sharps or flats, but C minor contains three flats.

Minor scales are broken up into three categories: natural, harmonic, and melodic.

Beginning on the root, the natural minor scale consists of the following intervals: whole, half, whole, whole, half, whole, whole. Take a look at A minor on the piano. This key uses all white notes. From A to B, there is a whole step. From B to C, there is a half step. From C to D, there is a whole step. From D to E, there is a whole step. From E to F, there is a half step. From F to G, there is a whole step, and from G to A, there is a whole step. This is shown to you in **FIGURE 4-6**.

FIGURE 4-6:
Ascending A
Natural Minor
Scale

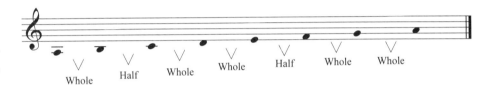

The harmonic minor is more exotic sounding, since it includes one accidental. Instead of playing a minor seventh, you will play a major seventh or leading tone. In the key of A minor, the harmonic scale will include a G sharp. **FIGURE 4-7** illustrates this.

FIGURE 4-7:
Ascending
A Harmonic
Minor Scale

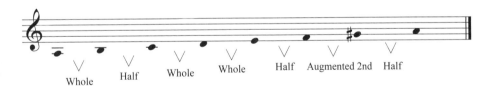

The melodic minor scale retains the minor third scale degree. However, it mimics a major scale on the sixth and seventh scale degrees. Traditionally, this occurs only when the scale ascends. In other words, the sixth and seventh scale degrees are altered only when you travel up the keyboard. When descending, the natural minor scale is used.

In the modern era, the melodic minor may be used when soloing over specific chord types. In this setting, it can be used when ascending and descending. The melodic minor scale is particularly effective when soloing over minor +7 chords (often called minor-major chords), suspended flat 9 chords, major +5 chords, dominant seventh +11 chords, half-diminished chords, and various "slash" chords. In this context, the pluses used above mean "sharp."

Minor keys have long been associated with sad and ominous music. Likewise, major keys have long been associated with sunny and uplifting music. There is some truth to these generalizations. However, far too many exceptions occur to label all minor-keyed songs "sad" and all major-keyed songs "happy."

The chords described above are very advanced. At this point, you are not expected to know what these chords mean or how to use them. However, they have been included for future reference. For now, just get acquainted with the melodic minor scale. **FIGURE 4-8** shows you an A melodic minor scale as it is written traditionally.

FIGURE 4-8:
Ascending and Descending A Melodic Minor Scale

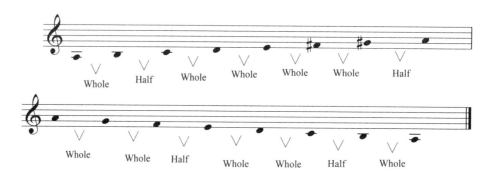

You should be fluent with the natural, harmonic, and melodic minor scales in all keys. However, documenting all three scales for all fifteen keys would require notating forty-five scales. Since this is beyond the scope of this book, **FIGURE 4-9** shows you the fingering and proper notation for the two minor scales used later in this text. They are C minor and A minor, respectively.

FIGURE 4-9: C Minor and A Minor Scales

TRACK 3

FIGURE 4-9 (continued): C Minor and A Minor Scales

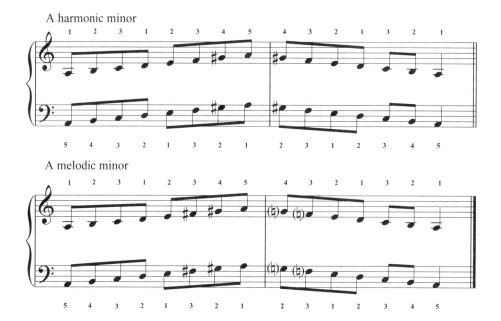

Using the Sustain Pedal

Grand pianos contain three pedals: sustain, sostenuto, and una corda. The sostenuto pedal allows only select notes to ring out. The una corda pedal shifts the hammers on the piano so that they strike only one or two of the strings rather than all three. The result is a muffled or softer sound.

The sustain pedal—also called the loud pedal, the forte pedal, or the damper pedal—has the widest applications in music. This pedal creates a full-bodied tone and allows pianists to play beautiful legato phrases.

On a grand piano, the sustain pedal is the pedal farthest to the right. It should be played with the ball of the foot while the heel rests comfortably on the floor. **FIGURE 4-10** shows you the order of all three pedals on the grand piano.

Pedaling on the sustain pedal comes down to three words: *before*, *with*, or *after*. Sometimes, you will want to anticipate your pedaling; you will press the pedal before you strike the keys. Other times, you will want to press the pedal as you strike the keys. Last, pianists will often strike the

FIGURE 4-10:
Una Corda,
Sostenuto, and
Sustain Pedals

una corda   sostenuto   forte/sustain

keys and then press the pedal; this is called syncopated pedaling. How do you know when to use each technique? It all depends on context, and in some cases, the composer's or songwriter's instructions. The bottom line is clarity. Always listen for this when you play.

QUESTION?

How does a sustain pedal work?
When you press down on the pedal, the dampening mechanism lifts so that the strings can vibrate freely. As a result, it's important to coordinate your playing with your pedaling. If your pedaling is sloppy, your playing will be sloppy. If you're not careful, unwanted notes will ring out and create ugly dissonances.

In written music, pedaling is indicated below the grand staff. There are different symbols used to denote pedaling. Sometimes, the abbreviation "*Ped.*" is used to indicate sustain. This is followed by an oversized asterisk, which tells you to lift up on the pedal. The use of "Ped." and brackets is also common. More and more, publishers are simply using brackets without the "Ped." abbreviation. This book uses brackets almost exclusively. For intricate pedaling, a fancier method is employed but this will be explained to you later. **FIGURE 4-11** shows you what the basic bracket method looks like.

FIGURE 4-11:
Pedaling Brackets

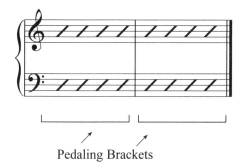

Pedaling Brackets

Blues styles like boogie-woogie and early rock-n-roll rarely use pedaling because the music is percussive and fast. Adding the sustain pedal to fast tempos often results in a washy mess. Pedaling is primarily used to add breadth and nuance to slow or sparse passages; chords, arpeggios, and melodic patterns all benefit from the sustain pedal. Be careful, however, when using the sustain pedal on music that contains lots of fast runs or complex rhythms. It can be used in these settings, but again, clarity must come first.

FACT

Upright pianos typically have una corda and sustain pedals, but manufacturers usually omit the sostenuto pedal. Digital pianos only use a sustain pedal, although some presets on today's keyboards include "una corda" sound. The sustain pedal is all you will need to play rock and blues music.

In this book, when pedaling is indicated on chords, you may either depress the pedal just after you strike the chord or while you strike the chord. For melodic patterns, you may depress the pedal just before the pattern or as you play the first note. It's important to listen to the way the pedal affects the flow of the music. The pedal should make each phrase sound rich and colorful. If it muddies up the sound, you need to improve your timing or omit the pedaling altogether.

Technique Builders

Practicing the scales is the best way to improve your mechanical skill and, overall, your ability to maneuver around the instrument. Rock and blues are both technically challenging styles of music. Whether you're playing a boogie-woogie bass line (Chapter 9) or progressive rock licks (Chapter 14), you will need to have fleet fingers.

One of the surest signs of a quality pianist is clean, articulate playing at fast tempos. The best way to develop finger technique is to practice scalar exercises. Thousands of permutations can be constructed out of the scales, and you can easily make up your own exercises to develop finger strength and control. After learning the technique builders in this chapter, try putting together your own patterns. When doing so, consider your weaknesses or deficiencies. For example, if you have an uncoordinated ring finger, create an exercise designed to give this finger a workout. Be sure to give equal time to each hand.

FIGURE 4-12 shows you one common scalar exercise. This is simply the C major scale played as continuous eighth notes. Because of the number of notes found in the scale, this pattern must be written in a mixed meter to maintain the rhythm. Use this idea on all of the major scales from **FIGURES 4-4** and **4-5**. You may also use it on the natural, harmonic, and melodic minor scales.

FIGURE 4-12:
C Major Scale
as Continuous
Eighth Notes

FIGURE **4-13** is an example of the scalar-based "motor" exercises described earlier. Here, the hands play in octaves up and down the keyboard. The pattern moves diatonically; in other words, it follows the C major scale and does not use "accidentals." Be sure to try this in all major and minor keys.

FIGURE 4-13: Scalar Technique Builder #1

TRACK 4

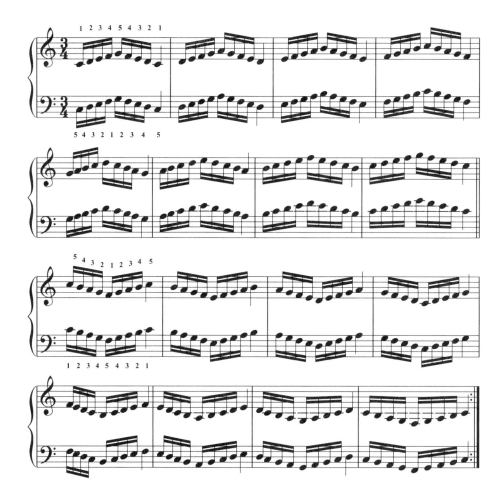

FIGURE 4-14 shows you a more complex scalar example. Like **FIGURE 4-13**, this exercise also revolves around the C major scale. Like the previous exercises, this pattern can be applied to all major and minor keys.

FIGURE 4-14: Scalar Technique Builder #2

TRACK 5

FIGURE 4-14 (continued): Scalar Technique Builder #2

FIGURE 4-15 is a more stationary exercise that uses major and minor keys (alternating between C major and its parallel minor). This pattern employs thirds, and again, your hands play in octaves. Fingering remains the same as the patterns shift. Memorize these exercises and use them as warm-ups.

Add depth to the technique builders by incorporating crescendos, decrescendos, and accents (see Chapter 10). Don't play too fast—play at a fast clip, but never sacrifice articulate and expressive playing for speed. If you feel pain in your tendons, take a break.

FIGURE 4-15: Scalar Technique Builder #3

TRACK 6

See "Arpeggios" on page 102 to find more exercises to build technique. For more scalar permutations, get the classic book *Hanon: The Virtuoso Pianist in Sixty Exercises for the Piano* by C. L. Hanon.

Chapter 5
Advanced Scales

This chapter introduces you to some practical scales, which can be used to play both rock and blues. On the following pages, you will learn about blues scales, pentatonic scales, chromatic scales, and other important modes. All of these scales will be applied to exercises and study pieces found later in the book. Because scales and chords cannot really be separated, you may want to reference Chapters 6 and 7 as you work your way through this chapter.

5

Blues Scales

The blues scale centers on blue notes. The most important blue notes are the flatted third and the flatted seventh. See **FIGURE 5-1**. In the key of C major, this would be E-flat and a B-flat, respectively. In the key of C major, an E-flat is a minor third and a B-flat is a minor seventh.

FACT

Tri-tones are very dissonant. Because of its jarring sound, this interval used to be called *diabolus in musica* (the devil's tone) during the Middle Ages.

The other blue note found in the blues scale is the flatted fifth. In some contexts, this interval is also written as an augmented fourth or sharp eleven. In the key of C major, the flatted fifth is a G-flat. When juxtaposed against C, the interval becomes a tri-tone.

FIGURE 5-1:
Blue Notes

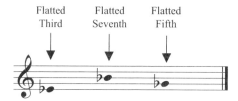

Early blues does not focus on the flatted fifth. It was occasionally used as a passing tone between the perfect fifth and the perfect fourth, or vice versa, but musicians rarely lingered on this note nor did they end phrases with it. However, jazz musicians, particularly bebop artists, made extensive use of this interval in the late 1940s and 1950s. For example, pianists such as Thelonious Monk regularly used the flatted fifth. **FIGURE 5-2** shows you a jazzy phrase with flatted fifths. This phrase mimics Monk's playing style.

The other notes in a basic blues scale include the tonic, the perfect fourth, and the perfect fifth. If you put all of these intervals together, the blues scale emerges. **FIGURE 5-3** shows you the basic blues scale written in C major.

FIGURE 5-2:
Using Flatted
Fifths

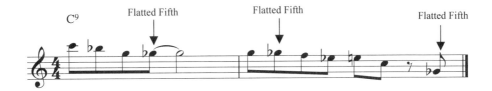

FIGURE 5-3:
Basic Blues
Scale

While the basic blues scale is useful, it is also limited. For example, a major third is often used in conjunction with the flatted third. **FIGURE 5-4** shows you this movement in the key of C major. Here, an E-flat slides into an E-natural.

FIGURE 5-4:
Minor Third–
Major Third Lick

Due to the limitations of the basic blues scale, a more comprehensive blues scale is needed to show the relationship between blue notes and other chord tones. In this scale, major second, major third, and major sixth scale degrees have been added. This is illustrated in **FIGURE 5-5**.

FIGURE 5-5:
Full Blues Scale

Memorize both the basic and the full blues scales. These scales will come up time and time again in this book. You will also make use of them in the blues study pieces found in Chapter 15.

Pentatonic Scales

A pentatonic scale is a five-note scale. This scale has wide applications in rock. Whether you're playing progressive rock or synth pop, new age or heavy metal, you will find this scale to be quite useful. Blues, R&B, and jazz musicians also use pentatonics quite effectively. From Delta blues to avant-garde jazz, this scale has seen a lot of action. For ultramodern applications of this scale, check out the playing styles of pianists McCoy Tyner and Mulgrew Miller.

In most cases, pentatonic scales are easy to use because they contain consonant intervals. *Consonance* refers to harmonic intervals that are euphonious or pleasing on the ear. *Dissonance* refers to harmonic intervals that are discordant, musically unstable, or demanding on the ear. Consonance and dissonance are relative terms.

As far as this book is concerned, melodic lines are always set against chords. Because of this, it's important to know what intervals fit well together. The bottom line is that pentatonics help you navigate your way around chord changes without too much worry. They are conservative scales, but they are very effective. They are also a great point of departure if you're a beginner learning how to improvise.

FIGURE 5-6 shows you one basic pentatonic scale written in the key of C major. The notes of this scale are C, D, E, G, and A. In other words, this scale comprises a root, a major second, a major third, a perfect fifth, and a major sixth. This is the most common pentatonic variety.

FIGURE 5-6: Basic
Pentatonic Scale

Four additional varieties exist. In no particular order, they are as follows:

- Root, second, fourth, fifth, and sixth (omitting the third)
- Root, second, fourth, fifth, and minor seventh (omitting the third and sixth)
- Root, minor third, fourth, fifth, and minor seventh
- Root, minor third, fourth, minor sixth, minor seventh (omitting the fifth)

These variations, including the two minor keyed versions, are notated in **FIGURE 5-7**. After you learn about harmony and accompaniment (Chapters 6 and 7), try combining these pentatonics with different chord types. Just remember: Never play minor pentatonics over major chords or vice versa.

FIGURE 5-7:
Pentatonic
Variations

The black keys on the piano (G-flat, A-flat, B-flat, D-flat, and E-flat) make up a pentatonic scale. Once you learn how to play a blues progression (Chapter 9), try soloing over a G-flat blues using only black keys. This is the easiest way to begin improvising. In this case, use triads as your accompaniment (Chapter 6).

If you wish to get a little more complex, try playing pentatonics over a C major blues. As you solo, shift the pentatonic scale to match each chord. This is shown in **FIGURE 5-8**. In this example, three chord types are listed: the I, IV, and V chords, respectively. As you can see, roman numerals are used to represent each chord.

FIGURE 5-8:
Pentatonics
over I, IV, and V
chords

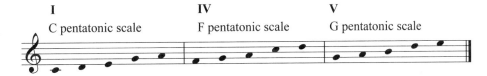

In general, pentatonics provide a wonderful springboard for improvisation. When soloing with pentatonics, or with any scale for that matter, mix up the order of the notes. You should not play straight-up, scalar lines; that is too mechanical and boring. Instead, use intervallic leaps to create memorable melodies and cool riffs.

Dorian Mode

Modes can be built off all seven pitches in the major scale. As stated earlier in the book, the C major scale is also known as the Ionian mode. This mode is built off the first scale degree in C major. Similarly, if you build a mode off the sixth scale degree in C major, you will get an Aeolian mode or A-natural minor scale.

If you build a scale off the second scale degree in C major, you will discover a versatile scale known as the D Dorian mode. The intervals in the Dorian mode are whole, half, whole, whole, whole, half, whole. In C major, this becomes D to E (whole), E to F (half), F to G (whole), G to A (whole), A to B (whole), B to C (half), and C to D (whole). This scale is written in **FIGURE 5-9**.

FIGURE 5-9: The
Dorian Mode

Like pentatonics, the Dorian mode is very effective and easy to use. The Dorian scale is almost always used over minor chords built on the second scale degree. In the key of C, this would be a D minor chord. As you will learn in Chapter 6, a minor triad rooted on D includes the notes D, F, and A. These notes, particularly the minor third, help define the Dorian mode. Additionally, this mode contains a major sixth. The major sixth is a critical feature of the Dorian mode. When you piece it all together, you will see that a Dorian mode is really just a natural minor scale with a raised (major) sixth. In fact, the Dorian mode uses the same notes as the natural minor scale located a perfect fourth below or a perfect fifth above the mode's root. For example, the notes in an A minor scale (A, B, C, D, E, F, G) match those of a D Dorian mode (D, E, F, G, A, B, C). The only difference is the starting pitches.

The Dorian mode is not limited to minor ii (two) chords. It can be used on the blues too. In its simplest form, the blues uses major triads built on the first, fourth, and fifth scale degrees (see Chapter 9). The Dorian mode can be used to solo over these chords provided you're careful to avoid certain perfect fourth intervals.

For example, in the key of C major, the I chord is a C major. Its chord tones are C, E, and G. The D Dorian scale can be used to solo over this chord, but you should generally avoid the note F since its relationship with C is a perfect fourth. In this context, it's best to navigate around perfect fouth intervals. The IV chord is an F major chord. Its chord tones are F, A, and C. Again, the D Dorian scale can be used on this chord. Here, you can play a B natural since it is an augmented fourth not a perfect fourth. (Raised fourths will be discussed later in the chapter.) The V chord contains the chord tones G, B, and D. Here, you may use the D Dorian mode, but you should avoid playing a C since it forms a perfect fourth with the root. The Dorian mode is paired up with the I, IV, and V chords in **FIGURE 5-10**.

FIGURE 5-10:

Dorian Mode over I, IV, and V Chords

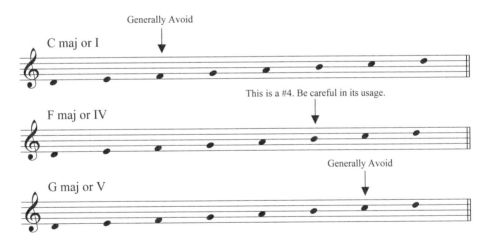

Once you add blue notes and/or other altered tones to the I, IV, and V chords, the Dorian scale becomes less handy. In other words, too many "avoid" notes crop up to warrant its use. Thankfully, there are other modes available, namely, the Mixolydian mode, the dominant scale, and the Lydian dominant mode. As you will see, all these scales have great blues applications.

As for other Dorian applications, use it freely on minor key modal jams. See "The Doors" section of Chapter 14 for an example. The Dorian mode gets a lot of use by artists who structure songs around a single minor chord or a series of minor chords. Miles Davis's "So What" is the perfect example. This tune contains only two minor chords: Dmin7 and E-flat min7. Progressions like these are fertile ground for Dorian modal explorations.

Mixolydian Mode

The Mixolydian mode uses the same intervals as the major scale with one very important exception. Instead of a leading tone, the seventh scale degree is flatted. For example, a G Mixolydian scale uses the notes G, A, B, C, D, E, F, and G. It does not use an F-sharp. This is shown in **FIGURE 5-11**.

FIGURE 5-11: G Mixolydian Mode

F natural

This scale has great applications in the blues since most blues chords use minor sevenths or, as this book sometimes calls them, dominant sevenths. The chords used in a simple C blues are C major, F major, and G major. However, most of the time, pianists will add flatted sevenths to create a dominant seventh chord. The Mixolydian scale fits beautifully over these kinds of chords since it also uses a flatted seventh. However, once again, you will need to be careful of the fourth scale degree since it creates a suspension. What are your options?

- Avoid the fourth scale degree altogether.
- Resolve the fourth scale degree down to a major third when you use it.
- Use it only as a passing tone in fast scalar runs.

One thing's for sure, never hang or linger on the perfect fourth on a dominant seventh chord. **FIGURE 5-12** shows you a suspended fourth resolving down to a major third. For more information on suspensions, including a definition of this term, see Chapter 7.

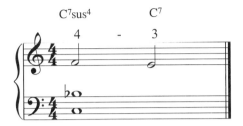

FIGURE 5-12:

Suspended
Fourth
Resolving to a
Major Third

Try playing the Mixolydian mode over I, IV, and V chords in C major as prep for playing the blues. Unlike the fourth scale degree, feel free to hang on flatted sevenths. Since this is a blue note, the flatted seventh will make your blues sound more authentic and even "down-home." **FIGURE 5-13** shows you Mixolydian modes in C, F, and G.

FIGURE 5-13:

Mixolydian
Modes over I, IV,
and V Chords

Be careful of the notes in ( ). See corresponding text.

The Dominant Scale and Chromatics

The dominant scale is basically the same as the Mixolydian mode. However, a leading tone has been added. This scale is popular with contemporary blues musicians, particularly those who play jazz. The leading tone completes a lengthy chromatic passage between the top four notes of the scale. Chromatics immediately invoke a jazzy flavor.

Chromatics are half step or semitone intervals. When you play chromatically, you strike every note on the keyboard—all white and black keys—as you move up or down the piano. With the exception of the whole tone scale, every scale uses some chromatics. However, the dominant scale uses enough successive chromatics to give this mode a distinctly jazzy feel.

From octave to octave, the dominant scale contains nine notes. For example, a C dominant scale consists of the notes C, D, E, F, G, A, B-flat, B, C. The movement between A, B-flat, B, and C is chromatic. This chromatic passage has been bracketed in **FIGURE 5-14**.

FIGURE 5-14: C
Dominant Scale

It's common for students to ask, "Why add the leading tone? What's its significance?" In addition to the lovely chromatic movement this produces, the leading tone also allows you to play chord tones on each downbeat. When you're a little more familiar with scales and the blues, play the I, IV, and V chords with your left hand as you run dominant scales with your right hand. After you are comfortable with this, play variations on the dominant scale by adding passing tones.

The first step is to choose a start point. Do not always begin on the root. Once you've picked a starting point, play eighth notes up or down the keyboard. It's more common to descend. As you do this, strike chord tones on the downbeats and nonchord tones (chromatics) on the upbeats.

Eighth notes divide the beat into two parts: an upbeat and a downbeat. The downbeat refers to rhythms played on the counted numbers: 1, 2, 3, and 4. An upbeat refers to the "ands" that make up the second part of the beat. Therefore, a measure of eighth notes is counted: 1-and, 2-and, 3-and, 4-and. Sometimes pluses (+) are used to indicate "ands."

The goal with this exercise is to find as many of the "hidden" chromatics as you can. Inevitably, you will end up playing some chord tones on "ands." This is okay. There are not always altered tones available to you on every upbeat. However, go slowly and grab as many of those passing tones as you can. Through this exercise, you will gain a sneak peek into the complex world of jazz improvisation. Ultimately, you will notice scalar combinations that you didn't know existed, and this will lead to the development of riffs and licks, which can be applied to blues and rock.

To get you started, **FIGURE 5-15** shows you the dominant scales for I, IV, and V chords in C major.

FIGURE 5-15:
Descending
Dominant
Scales over I, IV,
and V Chords

FIGURE 5-16 shows you some common errors that can be made when finding "hidden" chromatics. This example focuses on the IV chord. As you can see, the E-naturals played on the downbeats are mistakes. They are errors because they are not chord tones on an F7 chord. Strictly speaking, this chord contains only the notes F, A, C, and E-flat. In this context, an E-natural can be played *only* on an upbeat.

FIGURE 5-16:
Incorrect Scalar
Passage

A corrected version of **FIGURE 5-16** is shown in **FIGURE 5-17**. In this version, chord tones are maintained on all of the downbeats.

In the second measure of **FIGURE 5-17**, there is a chromatic movement that could be made between C and B-flat. A conscious decision was made not to do this because, as you know, it's best to offset the perfect fourth interval in a dominant seventh chord. Placing the B-flat on the upbeat de-emphasizes this interval. In this instance, it would not be wrong to place the B-flat on the downbeat (especially at fast tempos). However, it's best to play it on an upbeat when possible.

FIGURE 5-17:
Corrected Scalar
Passage

Last but not least, it's important to remember not to think of the leading tone in the dominant scale as a chord tone, even though it appears in the scale. In other words, do not play a B-natural on a downbeat over a C7. It should always be relegated to the upbeats just like its use in the scale. Of course, there are exceptions to these downbeat/upbeat rules. However, those exceptions go beyond the scope of this book. To learn more about this topic, you will need to study jazz theory.

Lydian Dominant

The Lydian dominant scale is another advanced concept used by contemporary blues musicians. This scale is a combination of the Lydian mode, which is a major scale with a raised fourth, and the dominant scale, which contains a flatted seventh. This scalar hybrid is shown to you in **FIGURE 5-18**.

Like the other scales in this chapter, the Lydian dominant can be used over I, IV, and V chords in a blues progression. **FIGURE 5-18** shows each scale in ascending order, indicating the raised fourths and flatted sevenths.

FIGURE 5-18:

Lydian
Dominant Scale

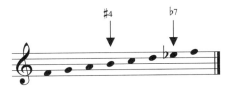

As you know, root/perfect fourth intervals don't complement dominant sevenths chords very well. The Lydian dominant takes care of this issue quite easily by using a raised fourth. The result is a tri-tone or, more specifically, an augmented fourth. In the context of music, this interval is usually called a sharp eleven, and it is the Lydian dominant's most prominent feature. When used appropriately, this interval adds an interesting melodic twist to blues riffs.

Often, Lydian dominant licks center around, and resolve to, the fifth scale degree. On a C7 chord, this resolution point is G. Lydian dominant riffs tend to embellish this scale degree quite effectively. **FIGURE 5-19** shows a common melodic twist that uses the Lydian Dominant scale. In this figure, a descending melody drops down to a sharp eleven. The melody then jumps up to a thirteenth before resolving on the consonant fifth.

FIGURE 5-19:

Lydian
Dominant
Scales over I, IV,
and V Chords

Another common Lydian dominant phrase uses grace notes (see Chapter 10) to slide into the sharp eleven of a V chord. From there, the line climbs back up until it lands on the fifth of the I chord. This is notated in **FIGURE 5-20**.

FIGURE 5-20:

Lydian Dominant Melodic Twist

FIGURES 5-20 and **5-21** are but two licks that use Lydian dominant. To hear the Lydian dominant mode used in a larger musical context, see **FIGURE 11-4**. Also, see **FIGURE 10-8** for note decorations that use the raised fourth.

FIGURE 5-21:

Another Common Lydian Dominant Melodic Turn

Chapter 6

Basic Harmony

Harmony is the cornerstone of all Western music, including rock and blues. In this chapter, you will learn harmony 101. Chord varieties will be discussed including major, minor, diminished, and augmented triads. You will also be introduced to dominant seventh chords. The chapter will end with a very important section on cadences. If you're interested in playing rock and pop music, you'll want to spend some extra time studying this section.

Major and Minor Triads

All of the chords in this book are called tertian chords. Tertian chords are essentially stacked thirds. Nothing epitomizes stacked thirds more than the basic triad. A triad has three notes; hence, the prefix *tri-*. You can call any three-note chord a triad. However, in Western music, a triad usually implies a root, a third, and a fifth. Major and minor triads are the most common examples, and they share two of the same notes. Specifically, the root and fifth of a major and minor triad are identical. For example, in the keys of C major and C minor, the root and fifth combination of C and G outlines a I chord; the difference between major and minor lies in the third scale degree.

QUESTION?

Why spell out a C minor triad with an E-flat rather than a D-sharp?
An E-flat and a D-sharp sound the same on a piano. However, an E-flat must be written if you are to create a minor third interval. The interval from C to D-sharp is an augmented second. D-sharp and E-flat are enharmonic partners.

As you might guess, the major triad contains a major third. If you're counting half steps or semitones, the major third is five steps away from the root. In C major, these steps are C (1), C-sharp (2), D (3), D-sharp (4), and E (5). As you know from Chapter 2, the relationship between a C and an E is a major third. The minor third contains only four half steps. This means that the third scale degree is flatted. In C major, the steps are C (1), C-sharp (2), D (3), and E-flat (4).

FIGURE 6-1 shows you a C major and a C minor triad. Again, the only difference between these chords is the third. You will see an E-natural in the C major triad and an E-flat in the C minor triad.

FIGURE 6-1:
C Major and C
Minor Triads

Since these chords contain three notes, they can be written with three different roots. When C is in the bottom, as in **FIGURE 6-1**, the chords are in root position. When the third is in the bottom, these chords are in first position. When the fifth is in the bottom, these chords are written in second position. In general terms, first and second positions are called inversions.

FACT

In baroque music, inversions would be notated using figured bass. Figured bass is a numeral system used to tell musicians how to voice chords in relationship to a bass line. Although this method of notation is still widely used in music theory classes, it has little application to blues, rock, and pop music.

FIGURE 6-2 shows you major and minor triadic inversions in C major and C minor. Questions will inevitably arise, such as how do you know what inversion(s) to use, and when. It all depends on voice leading and musical context. For more on this topic, see the "Chord Voicings" section in Chapter 12.

FIGURE 6-2: Major and Minor Triadic Inversions

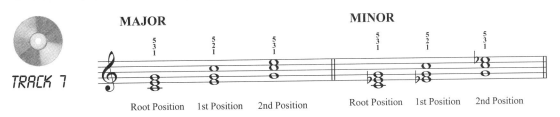

TRACK 7

Diatonic Triads of the Major Scale

If you build a triad off each scale degree in a major scale, you get three types of chords. They are major, minor, and diminished, respectively. Simply stack thirds to create each chord. **FIGURE 6-3** illustrates this in the key of C major.

The chords in the figure are spelled out in root position; roman numerals indicate each chord variety. Notice how the minor and diminished chords

FIGURE 6-3: Diatonic Triads of the Major Scale

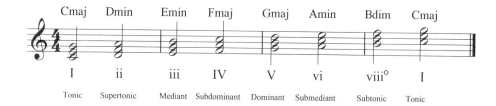

are spelled out using lower-case numerals; this is standard in Western musical notation.

Like all chords, the triads of the major scale may be inverted. In each case, the chord will invert exactly as indicated in **FIGURE 6-2**. This means that there are two inversions per chord. For example, a vi chord (A minor) can be inverted as such:

FIGURE 6-4: vi Chord Inversions

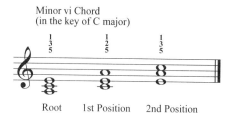

At this stage, your job is to become acquainted with each diatonic triad. These chords are the basis for thousands of chord progressions in thousands of songs. Once you learn them in C major, try them in other keys as well. At the end of this chapter, and later in Chapter 12, you will see how these chords can be combined to create practical chord progressions.

Dominant Seventh Chords

Dominant seventh chords are used a lot in rock and pop music, and they are the veritable backbone of the blues. This is because the dominant seventh chord contains a blue note. Specifically, this chord features a flatted seventh. As you learned in Chapter 5, the flatted seventh is an important interval in blues music. When a dominant seventh chord is written in sheet music, the word *dominant*, or the abbreviation *dom*, is not included. Instead, the chord will contain a letter name and the number seven. For example, you will see C7, G7, or B7.

Advanced players may interpret dominant seventh chords in a variety of ways. This usually means omitting certain chord tones and adding fancy chord extensions. However, as a beginner, you should first learn how to play these chords without embellishment.

All you need to remember is that a dominant seventh chord contains a major triad plus a flatted seventh on top. Once you add the flatted seventh, you will have a four-note chord, and therefore, you can create three possible inversions. **FIGURE 6-5** shows you a C7 chord and its inversions.

FIGURE 6-5: C7 Chord and Its Inversions

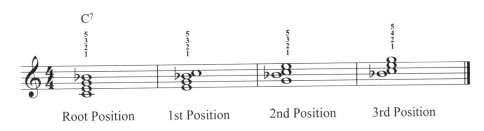

Root Position   1st Position   2nd Position   3rd Position

Pianists often play the root of a chord in the left hand (bass) while the right hand plays the remaining three chord tones. This is illustrated in **FIGURE 6-6**.

FIGURE 6-6: C7 Chord Interpreted on the Piano

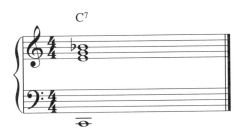

You may also offset a C7, or any other chord for that matter, between the hands. When you do this, new rhythms result. The most basic way to break up chords is to use quarter and/or eighth notes. This is demonstrated in the figure. Bear in mind, that other rhythms may be used as well including triplets or "swing eighths."

FIGURE 6-7: C7 Chord Broken Up Between the Hands

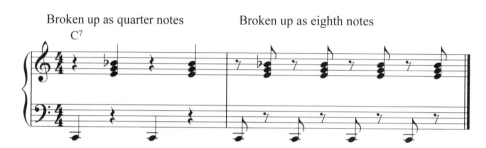

Shell voicings are also used when playing chords. A shell voicing contains only select chord tones. It's called a shell because it is not a full chord. Rather, it is an outline of a chord. You may be wondering, "If it's an outline of a chord, which notes are omitted?" Note omissions are left to the discretion of the pianist and decisions are made based on musical context. One common shell voicing for a C7 chord contains only the notes C and B-flat. Another contains only the notes E and B-flat. This is shown in **FIGURE 6-8**. Shell voicings will be discussed again in Chapter 9.

FIGURE 6-8: C7 Shell Voicings

Diminished, Half-Diminished, and Augmented Chords

Diminished chords naturally occur on the leading tone (subtonic) of a major scale. For example, in the key of C major, a diminished chord is rooted on B, the seventh scale degree. The diminished chord contains a double minor third interval. In other words, two minor thirds are stacked on top of each other to create the diminished chord quality. A B-diminished chord contains the intervals B to D (minor third) and D to F (minor third). If it were a minor chord, the F would be sharp.

A B-diminished chord is shown to you in **FIGURE 6-9**. As you will see, a circle is used to indicate the chord quality.

FIGURE 6-9:
B Diminished
Chord

Diminished seven chords are typically used as a substitute for V chords. As unstable chords, they naturally lean in the direction of the tonic. A diminished seven stacks another minor third interval on top of the root, making the interval between the root and seventh enharmonically the same as a major sixth. For example, a B dim7 chord contains an A-flat on top. If written as a G-sharp, the interval will be a major sixth.

FACT

The diminished chord gets its name from the interval created between the root and the flatted fifth. As you might guess, this interval between these two scale degrees is a diminished fifth.

Don't be confused by enharmonic naming. Just remember that a diminished seventh chord contains three stacked minor third intervals. Also, bear in mind that if you wish to use a diminished triad in place of a five chord, you might instead choose a diminished seven chord as it is more colorful. The diminished seven is shown in **FIGURE 6-10**.

FIGURE 6-10:
Diminished
Seven Chord

In **FIGURE 6-11**, the diminished seven chord is put to use in a simple chord progression. In this progression, the diminished seven and a flatted fifth are used to alter what could be a minor ii chord into a diminished seventh chord. By altering the perfect fifth of the chord to a flatted fifth, the diminished triad reveals itself. The staggered C-flat completes the picture by adding a diminished seventh on top.

FIGURE 6-11: Using a Diminished Seven Chord

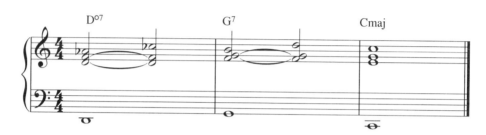

Half-Diminished Chord

The half-diminished chord is a rather beautiful, impressionistic chord that can be used in a variety of ways. It is mostly used in modern jazz and European classical music (late romantic and twentieth-century periods). However, it can be applied to pop and rock music, adding a resplendent glow to otherwise stock chord progressions. For example, jazz-rock groups like Steely Dan might use this chord as a fancy minor ii. In this case, a V and a I chord usually follow suit.

Often spelled out as a minor seven-flat five, the half-diminished chord contains most of the same notes as a full-diminished seventh chord. The exception lies in the seventh itself. Instead of stacked minor thirds, the half diminished contains a major third on top. For example, a B half diminished contains the notes B, D, F, and A. The relationship between F and A is a major third. The half-diminished chord is notated in **FIGURE 6-12**. As you will see, the symbol for half diminished is a circle with a line or slash through it.

FIGURE 6-12: Half-Diminished Chord

To create a fancy version of a standard ii–V–I chord progression, you can alter the minor ii chord to become a half diminished. This kind of harmonic twist is common in jazz. **FIGURE 6-13** shows one example of how to do this.

FIGURE 6-13:
Using a Half-Diminished Chord

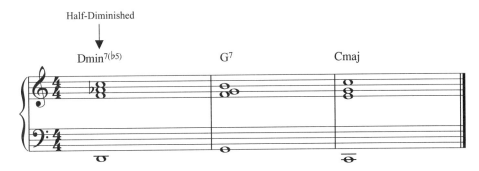

Augmented Chord

The augmented chord is a major triad with a sharp five. For example, a C-augmented chord would contain the notes C, E, and G-sharp. Enharmonically, this G-sharp is also an A-flat. As an A-flat, this interval would be called a flatted thirteenth. Like the half-diminished chord, the augmented chord is used primarily in jazz and contemporary classical, but it could also have applications in rock and pop. You will definitely see and hear it used in the blues examples found later in the book. **FIGURE 6-14** shows you a C-augmented chord and a C-augmented seven chord. A C-augmented chord is usually written as C7♯5 or C+7. The "+" symbol indicates the presence of a sharp five. Usually, augmented seven chords are used to spice up V chords.

FIGURE 6-14:
C-Augmented and C-Augmented Seven Chords

FIGURE 6-15 shows you a fancy version of a standard ii–V–I chord progression. In this figure, the V chord has been altered to become an augmented

seven chord. Listen to how the augmented chord changes the color and feel of this stock progression.

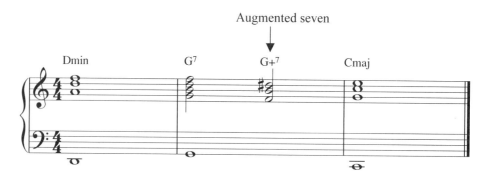

FIGURE 6-15: Using an Augmented Seven Chord

Secondary Dominant Chords

Secondary dominant chords are "V of __" Chords. When using roman numerals, secondary dominants are spelled out using slashes. For example, you might see a V/V. This tells you to play the major chord that is five scale degrees above the dominant chord. In the key of C major, this translates to mean D major and G major, respectively; D is a perfect fifth above G.

ALERT!

Secondary dominant chords do not work well when paired with the seventh (leading tone) scale degree. This is because the seventh scale degree forms a diminished triad, which is highly unstable. The secondary dominant should also never be associated with a I or tonic chord since the V of I is a primary dominant chord.

Secondary dominant chords are not limited to V chords. **FIGURE 6-16** shows you all of the secondary dominant chords you may use to spice up your chord progressions. In addition to V/V, you will see V/ii, V/iii, V/IV, and V/vi chords. In order to allow these chords to flow smoothly from one to the next, inversions have been used.

FIGURE 6-16:
Secondary
Dominant
Chords

Inversions allow each chord to flow easily into the next.

Secondary dominants are interesting passageways between two diatonic triads. This is illustrated in **FIGURE 6-17**. Here, a V of ii spices up a simple I–ii–V7–I chord progression.

FIGURE 6-17:
Secondary
Dominant
Chord
Progression

Borrowed Chords

Borrowed chords employ chords from the parallel key. For example, if you're in C major, the parallel minor key is C minor. This is not to be confused with the term *relative minor*. Relative keys refer to keys that share the same sharps and flats. For example, C major and A minor are relative keys, not parallel keys.

Borrowed chords can add excitement to any chord progression. Unlike some of the other chords described in this chapter, borrowed chords don't merely enhance a chord—they are not harmonic extensions or alterations like sevenths or sharp fives. Instead, borrowed chords bend the ear in another direction entirely, taking the listener in an unanticipated harmonic direction.

Flat VI and flat VII chords are wonderful examples of borrowed chords. **FIGURE 6-15** shows you an approach to C major (I chord) using both the flat VI and the flat VII. In this example, diatonic VI and VII chords from C minor are used. You will see this progression used again in **FIGURE 15-7**, Pop Etude: "For Kicks."

FIGURE 6-18:
Borrowed Chords

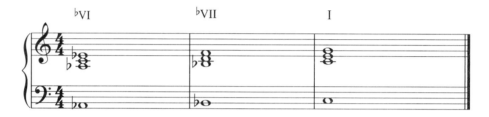

Among others, the Beatles used borrowed chords effectively. Songs such as "If I Fell" and "In My Life" used minor iv borrowed chords throughout. In **FIGURE 6-16**, two minor iv borrowed chord progressions are written out for you. Again, the minor iv comes from the parallel key not the relative key. In this instance, the two keys used are C major and C minor.

FIGURE 6-19:
Minor iv Borrowed
Chord

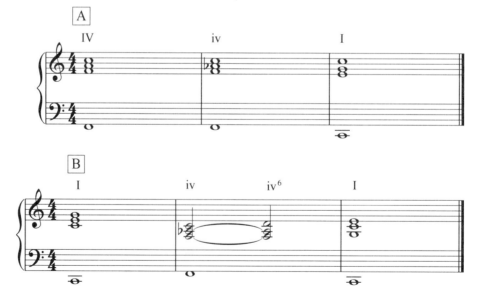

Types of Cadences

A cadence is a series of chords that signal the end or closing of a phrase. Cadences are also found at the conclusion of a piece of music. Some cadences are obvious to listeners because they begin and end on I chords. However, songs needn't always fit this mold. In fact, it's refreshing when a piece of music doesn't use obvious cadences. Still, cadences are necessary since they bring needed resolution. Without cadences, chords will simply hang in the air and there will be no musical closure. Listeners' ears crave the resolution and finality that cadences provide.

FIGURE 6-20 details the four standard cadences. However, many more cadences can be found in music. The following list is by no means complete. As your ear develops, listen for other cadences in rock and blues (and other styles of music for that matter).

The most important cadences in modern music are authentic, half, plagal, and deceptive.

The authentic and plagal cadences are the most common cadences in Western music, followed by the deceptive cadence, which is also quite universal. As you will learn in Chapter 9, the blues is built around authentic and plagal cadences since it uses I, IV, and V chords so extensively.

FIGURE 6-20: Standard Cadences

TRACK 9

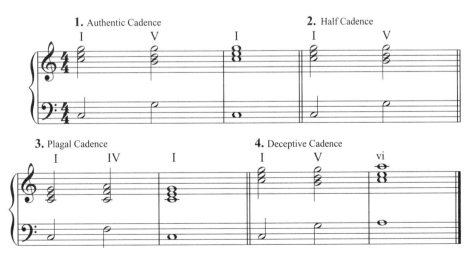

You may also add sevenths to the V chords in these cadences.

The authentic cadence is a simple chordal movement from V to I. The half cadence is a cadence that never resolves to a I chord. Instead, it hangs on a V chord indefinitely. Sometimes you will hear pop songs that end on V chords. Another type of half cadence is the Phrygian cadence. However, this cadence is not included here since it applies mostly to baroque music.

The plagal cadence moves from IV to I. This cadence is also known as the "Amen" cadence since it is used to sing "amen" in churches. The deceptive cadence is similar to the authentic cadence. However, instead of resolving on a I chord, it deceives the ear, and lands on a minor vi.

FIGURE 6-21 shows you some examples of other more contemporary cadences. In most cases, these cadences do not have official names. Nonetheless, they are found in many styles of music, especially pop and rock.

The first cadence found in **FIGURE 6-21** is a standard diminished cadence. Since the diminished vii chord functions in much the same way as a V7 chord, you can use it as a chordal substitution when playing an authentic cadence. The Neapolitan major and minor cadences are more antiquated. Yet, Neapolitan chords have an interesting color, and you can use them in pop and rock music. Neapolitan chords are especially useful in prog-rock since this substyle of music mimics the baroque and classical eras.

Cadences 4 and 5 from **FIGURE 6-21** use borrowed chords to add a distinct harmonic twist to the plagal cadence. Last, the chord progressions illustrated in 7 and 8 of **FIGURE 6-21** use slash chords. Slash chords are really just triads with substitute bass notes. See how you can apply all of these cadences to songs you may be writing. If you use them wisely, your music will not only be well grounded, it will be filled with great color and variety.

FIGURE 6-21: Other Practical Cadences

TRACK 10

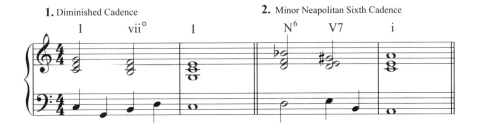

Note: This figure does *not* conform to the rules of four-part choral writing.

Chapter 7

Extensions, Suspensions, Passing Chords, and More

This chapter concentrates on harmonic extensions such as major and minor sevenths, ninths, and thirteenths. You will also learn about suspended chords, which are a staple in pop music. Last, you will learn about chromatic passing chords. These chords will add a jazzy flair to any I, IV, V blues. If you're looking to expand your harmonic horizons, read on. This chapter contains a whole host of colorful chords. As musicians would say, you'll learn about all the "hip changes" here.

Major and Minor Seven Chords

Major and minor seven chords can be used to add color to basic triads. In Chapter 6, you learned that stacking a minor seventh onto a major triad produced a dominant seventh chord. Now, try stacking a major seventh onto a major triad. This will produce a chord called the major seven.

Major seven chords add jazziness to a musical passage. Alone, a major seventh interval can sound ugly. For example, try playing a middle C or C4 followed by a B4 on the piano. Remember, B4 is located above C4. (It is not the B adjacent to C4.) When you play these notes together, the interval sounds dissonant and unstable. However, when a major third and a perfect fifth are present, the major seventh lays quite beautifully on top. This is because the major seventh is a natural extension in the overtone series. **FIGURE 7-1** shows you both a major seven interval and the C major seven chord in root position.

FIGURE 7-1:
Major Seven
Interval and Chord

Like triads and dominant seventh chords, major seven chords can also be inverted. **FIGURE 7-2** shows you a major seven chord in root position followed by its three inversions. It is written in the key of C major.

FIGURE 7-2: C
Major Seven Chord
Inversions

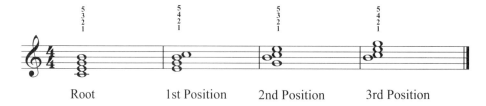

Root   1st Position   2nd Position   3rd Position

Unlike their minor counterparts, major seven chords have a warm, fuzzy quality. As a result, the major seven chord is used quite effectively in upbeat, cheery pop music. **FIGURE 7-3** shows you a two-chord pop progression that uses major sevenths. Notice the use of roots and fifths in the bass line; this is a common practice.

FIGURE 7-3:
Major Seven
Pop Chord
Progression

Minor seven chords have a darker sound. Much of this is due to the flatted third interval. Like the major seven chord, the minor seven is based on stacked thirds; since it's a four-note chord, it also has three inversions. **FIGURE 7-4** shows a minor seven interval rooted on C and a C minor seven chord in root position. As you will see, a minor seven interval also outlines a dominant seventh chord. However, once the minor third enters into the picture, the chord's quality becomes well defined.

FIGURE 7-4:
Minor Seven
Interval and
Chord

Like any other chord, minor seven chords can also be inverted. **FIGURE 7-5** shows this chord in root position together with its inversions written in C minor. Be sure to note the fingerings, but remember that they may not transfer to other keys.

FIGURE 7-5:
C Minor Seven
Chord Inversions

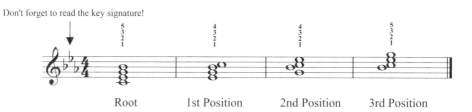

Minor seven chords are useful when playing a minor blues. **FIGURE 7-6** shows you the first eight measures of a C minor blues. The left hand is playing a walking bass line, which you will learn more about in Chapter 9, and the right hand is playing inversions of C minor seven and F minor seven chords respectively. These chords make up the minor i and minor iv chords of a minor blues.

FIGURE 7-6: Using Minor Seven Chords in the Blues

TRACK 11

Major and Minor Nine Chords

Ninths are also common harmonic extensions. Major nine and minor nine chords are generally interchangeable with their major and minor seven counterparts. In each case, the nine simply adds another color or harmonic texture on top of the seventh. **FIGURE 7-7** shows a major nine interval, a major nine chord, and a minor nine chord, respectively.

FIGURE 7-7:
Major Nine
Interval, Major
Nine Chord,
and Minor Nine
Chord

One common minor nine inversion allows for a half step to occur between the major second interval (usually called the major ninth) and the minor third interval. When in this position, the minor seven interval is found on the bottom of the chord. For example, from bottom to top, a Gmin9 would be voiced as such: F, A, B-flat, and D. As you can see, the minor seventh (F) is on the bottom of the chord. Plus, A and B-flat create a lovely half-step interval that adds just the right dissonance to the chord. What about the root? The root (G) is not included in the voicing. Instead, it is played in the left hand.

In today's world, all styles of music are blending as new hybrids arise. Given this, don't be afraid to use Latin elements (such as the Brazilian bossa nova) in your pop or rock songs. In general, use minor nine chords whenever you want to add an elegant or classy feel to your music.

When voiced in this manner, the minor nine chord sounds moody yet enchanting. Because of this, the minor nine is perfect for romantic songs or jazzy interludes.

Take the previously described Gmin9 chord and pair it with a Bmin9. Now try adding a groovy bossa nova bass line using roots and fifths. The result is quite striking.

FIGURE 7-8: Using Inverted Minor Nine Chords

TRACK 12

Major ninth intervals are useful when playing the blues, and they are used a great deal in both major and minor keys. For example, revisit the minor blues excerpt in **FIGURE 7-6**. If you add a major ninth interval to the I and IV chords—C minor and F minor, respectively—the progression will get a little more sophisticated and chic. **FIGURE 7-7** shows you how to do this.

FIGURE 7-9: Using Minor Nine Chords in the Blues

TRACK 13

Using major nine intervals on a *major* blues is also common. However, a thirteenth is usually added to support the chord. **FIGURE 7-10** shows you fancy I, IV, and V chords in C major. As you will learn in Chapter 9, I, IV, and V chords are the building blocks of the blues. In **FIGURE 7-10**, these spiced up I, IV, and V chords all contain the following:

- Major third
- Major sixth (usually called a thirteenth)
- Minor seventh (or as this book sometimes calls it a "dominant" seventh)
- Major ninth

Notice how the root of each chord is played only in the bass. After you learn the elements of the blues in Chapter 9, try substituting triads and simple shell voicings with the more dissonant chords in **FIGURE 7-10**. When doing so, listen to see when these chords work and when they seem excessive or too harsh. Usually, their use depends on the style of blues you're playing. These chords are particularly effective in jazz blues and other contemporary blues hybrids.

FIGURE 7-10:
Ninth-
Thirteenth
Chords

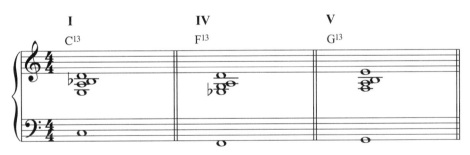

Even though ninths are found in these chords, they are usually written as 13 chords and the nine is implied.

Suspended Chords

Suspensions are used a great deal by pop and jazz pianists. Suspensions allow a chord to hang in the air, as it were, adding subtle tension and release to a musical passage. Suspensions usually last only a beat or two. When they do resolve, the resolution is more pronounced and noticeable. If applied properly, suspensions will make any chord progression more attractive to the ear. Needless to say, suspensions are a must if you plan on playing any kind of popular music.

There are two types of suspensions.

1. Suspended seconds (sus2)
2. Suspended fourths (sus4)

This means that, in lieu of a major or minor third, a chord will contain the second scale degree or the fourth scale degree. In all cases, the chord will appear to "suspend" or freeze in time before it resolves to the tonic or major third. It is more common for suspensions to resolve to the major third because of the widespread use of suspended fourths.

FIGURE 7-11 shows you a variety of suspended second and suspended fourth chords in C major. The first example moves from a suspended second (D) to a major third (E). The second example moves from a suspended second (D) to the tonic (C). The third scale degree is not even used in this example. The next example moves from a suspended fourth (F) to a major third (E), and the last example incorporates both a suspended second (D) and a suspended fourth (F). In this case, the chord eventually resolves to a major third (E).

FIGURE 7-11:
Types of Suspensions

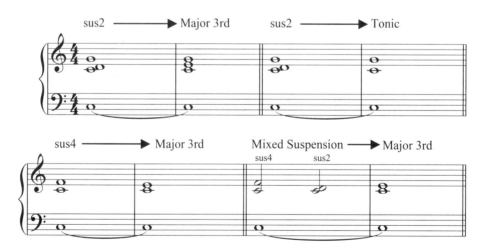

As mentioned earlier, some suspensions never resolve. Instead, they merely float over the music. In this case, songwriters might choose to use a series of suspended chords to keep the mood and character of the chord progression consistent. **FIGURE 7-12** is a loop of two suspended chords. Never do these chords resolve. In fact, they sound as though they could go on forever. Unresolved suspensions add intrigue and suspense to music. As a result, movie soundtracks tend to favor them. Also, if you put an electronic backbeat behind unresolved suspended chords, an ordinary dance beat will quickly turn into a sleek groove.

FIGURE 7-12: Unresolved Suspensions

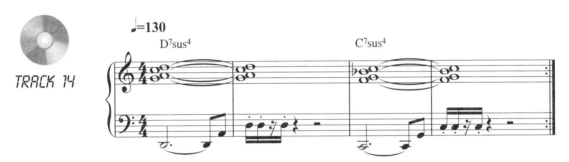

TRACK 14

Folk, pop, country, and new age artists also use suspensions a lot. However, they typically resolve each suspension. In **FIGURE 7-13**, you will see a miniature version of a typical pop ballad. As you might guess, this ballad uses many suspensions. Count the number of suspensions found in this example. *Hint:* There are four. (Suspended twos occur on beat one of measures one and two. A suspended fourth occurs on beat one of the third measure, and a suspended two occurs on beat one of the fourth measure.)

FIGURE 7-13: Pop Ballad with Suspensions

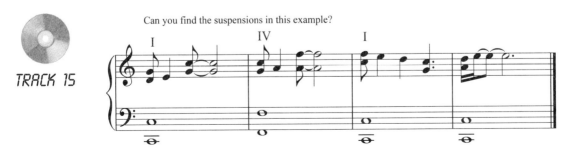

TRACK 15

In general, suspensions "soup" up run-of-the-mill chords. Don't be afraid to experiment with suspended twos and fours in your own music. They add just the right twist to ordinary triads and seventh chords.

FACT

In jazz and contemporary classical, suspended chords might never resolve. Instead, they float over the music like beautiful harmonic pastels. Rock, folk, country, and pop music almost always resolve suspensions. Either way, suspensions are an important chordal decoration that adds to the charm and variety of a song's chord progression.

Altered Dominant Chords

Altered dominant chords are used in both rock and blues. They are particularly effective when playing major and minor blues. As you know, the dominant chord is built on the fifth scale degree. Therefore, it is called a V chord. Instead of playing a V chord (triad) or a V7 (dominant seventh), try adding sharp nines and flat nines. Once you do, your chord will contain an accidental. Therefore, it becomes an altered dominant. **FIGURE 7-14** shows a sharp nine and a flat nine set against the note G. This note was chosen because, in the key of C major, a G is the root of a V chord.

Another altered tone used to spruce up V chords is the flatted thirteenth. **FIGURE 7-15** shows a flatted thirteenth set against the note G.

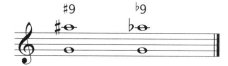

FIGURE 7-14: Sharp Nine and Flat Nine

FIGURE 7-15: Flat Thirteen

Additionally, you may flat the fifth scale degree as discussed in Chapter 5. In general, when you play a V chord, you may choose between four altered tones: flat fives, sharp nines, flat nines, and flat thirteens. **FIGURE 7-16** shows some common altered chords. In literal intervallic terms, the flatted thirteenth will often appear as a flatted sixth. However, musical convention dictates that this extension is typically referred to as a flat thirteen.

FIGURE 7-16:
Altered
Dominant
Chords

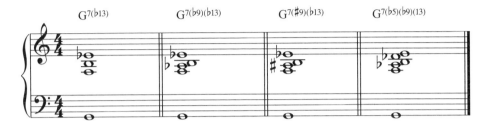

When you play the chords in **FIGURE 7-16**, you will realize that they are quite dissonant. Therefore, you have to be careful in applying these chords. When playing a jazz blues (in a major key), altered dominants can add extra dimension and sophistication to your chordal palette. However, beware! These chords are not appropriate for all blues settings. For example, traditional styles of blues, such as Delta and Chicago blues, would never (or very rarely) use such complex chords. The bottom line is to be mindful when applying fancy chords to any song. When doing so, trust your ear. If anything, the first chord in **FIGURE 7-16** is the most practical. The other chords are more eccentric, but they do have their place in more sophisticated milieus.

Sharp Nines and Flat Nines

In a minor blues, it is common to use a sharp nine on the V chord. For example, in the key of A minor, the V chord is E major. However, in a minor blues, basic V triads and V7 chords can sound hokey. It is more idiomatic to play the thirteenth chord that is located a tri-tone—augmented fourth or diminished fifth—above the root of the V chord. In the key of A minor, this means that you will play a B flat thirteen chord over an E root. The G creates a sharp nine.

This practice is used very often in minor blues. For example, listen to the music of Stevie Ray Vaughan, the late legendary Texas guitarist. Vaughan loved minor blues. When his band played them, they played sharp nines on V chords just about every time.

> When playing walking bass lines (see Chapter 9) over sharp nine chords, the bass pattern must contain a diminished fifth—not a perfect fifth. Perfect fifths don't sound as good in this musical context. For example, on a V7♯9 chord in A minor, you should use B flats in your bass line, not B naturals.

How do you voice sharp nine chords? There are several options depending on context. Here's one: In A minor, the V chord is E7♯9 and it should contain the notes: G sharp, D, and G natural. (The G natural is the sharp nine.) When voicing this chord, the root (E) should be played only in the bass (left hand). When resolving this chord, it is common to move from the sharp nine to the flat nine—in this case an F—before resolving neatly on the minor i⁹ chord.

This voicing is shown to you in **FIGURE 7-17**. Notice how the bass moves from an E to a B flat (a tri-tone). Since the pairing of a minor blues with a sharp nine V chord is so common, a full minor blues has been provided for you in **FIGURE 7-18**. This blues uses sharp nines and flat nines on all the V chords. Since the main objective of this figure is to introduce you to this concept, the V chord is held out on measures nine and ten. However, on measure ten, you could also play a IV chord (Dmin9). If you're new to blues music, you might want to skip this figure and come back to it after you've learned the elementary blues material in Chapter 9. Otherwise, be sure to

FIGURE 7-17: Using Sharp Nines and Flat Nines

FIGURE 7-18: Minor Blues with Sharp Nines and Flat Nines

TRACK 16

invoke this rule when you are asked to play a blues in a minor key. If you do, your playing will sound much more idiomatic and fluent.

Chromatic Passing Chords

Chromatic passing chords follow the same basic rules as single chromatic passing tones. In Chapter 5, you learned about the dominant scale, which uses chromatic movement between the tonic and the flatted seventh. You also learned that nonscale tones—also called altered tones—should only be played on upbeats or *ands*.

Since chords rarely move in eighth notes, you will play chromatic passing chords on the downbeats two and four. These are the weak beats in 4/4 time.

In a traditional blues setting, passing chromatic chords will most likely be played in a descending order from V to IV or from flat II to I. When used properly, passing chromatics give a distinct "falling" effect. They allow for a smooth transition between diatonic chords, and they also add a velvety sheen to the music.

ALERT!

As you learn about chromatic passing chords, you may want to refer to Chapter 9, which includes crucial information on blues structure. You cannot use passing chords until you first understand the basic chord and bar structure of the blues.

FIGURE 7-19 shows you a chromatic passing chord between V and IV chords in C major. Only triads in root position have been used here; you will see that the passing chord is nothing more than a flat V chord. In other words, in this example, the V chord contains the notes G, B, and D. The passing chord contains the notes G-flat, B-flat, and D-flat. Also notice how this chord is played on beat four: a weak beat.

FIGURE 7-19:
Moving
Chromatically
Between V and IV

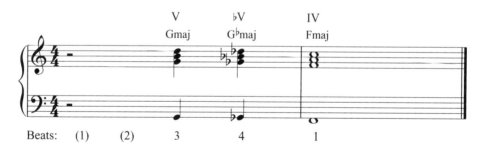

Next, try moving chromatically between V and IV using thirteen chords. See **FIGURE 7-20**. These chords are very effective in a jazz blues setting. Notice how each thirteen chord contains a third, seventh, and ninth. Additionally, the root is played only in the bass.

FIGURE 7-20:

Moving
Chromatically
Between V
and IV Using
Thirteen Chords

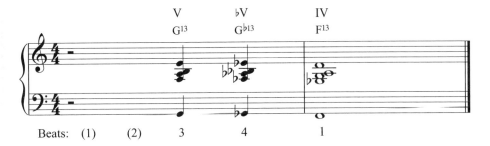

You can also move chromatically between flat II and I. See **FIGURE 7-21**. When this occurs, you will be at the end of the blues form. In other words, you'll be coming off a V chord and moving into the start of a new chorus. (For a definition of *chorus*, see Chapter 9.) In this situation, the flat II chromatic passing chord

FIGURE 7-21:

Moving
Chromatically
Between V, Flat
II, and I

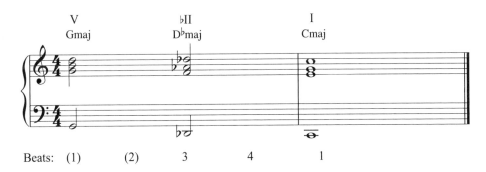

merely acts as a transition between the V and the I chord. Here, chromatic movement is used between the top notes or highest pitches in each chord.

The movement from V to flat II to I is a little smoother and more interesting when you add extensions and altered tones. Make sure the top notes of each chord move chromatically. **FIGURE 7-22** invokes this kind of chromatic

FIGURE 7-22:

Moving
Chromatically
Between V, Flat
II, and I Using
Extensions and
Altered Tones

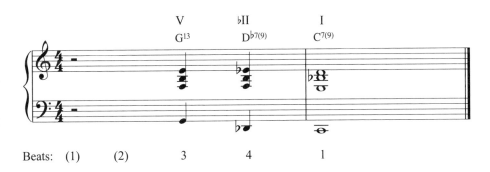

movement in the top voice. As you will see, E (thirteenth), E-flat (ninth), and D (ninth) create this desired chromatic effect.

Last, you can leave the V chord out altogether. On the last measure of the blues, musicians often will play a V chord, creating an authentic cadence between I and V. However, you may leave this out entirely and play a flat II chord on either beat three or beat four of the measure. This works best when using inverted chords or harmonic extensions since chromatic movement is desired between the top notes of each chord.

FIGURE 7-23:
Moving
Chromatically
Between I and
Flat II

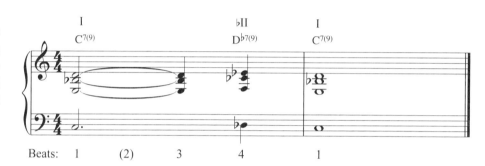

Once you become more acquainted with the blues in Chapters 9, 10, and 11, you may want to return to this chapter to review some of the chord varieties described here. Always use your ear when experimenting with fancy chords. Sometimes, notes in the melody clash with notes in the chords, so you must be careful and judicious in your use of dissonant chord types.

Chapter 8

Combining Chords and Scales and Arpeggios

It's time to put together scales with chords to pave the way for soloing and song writing. This chapter should be referenced with the scales in Chapter 5 since it draws heavily from the information you learned there. The harmonic minor scale, the Dorian mode, major and minor pentatonics, blues scales, and the dominant and Lydian dominant scales will be set against chords in this chapter. You will also be introduced to arpeggios, which are really just broken chords.

8

Combining Chords with Scales

Melody and harmony are lovely on their own. However, they are only components and, therefore, are limited. To fully experience the richness of music, you must combine melody and harmony. More specifically, you must know what chords go with what scales. If you don't, you'll never be able to solo well or to write songs that are pleasing to the ear. Even the most uneducated listeners can tell when a musician plays blatantly "wrong" notes. The listeners may not be able to articulate what they don't like about the pianist, but they will subconsciously detect that the performer just doesn't know how to combine melody and harmony to create mellifluous, ear-catching musical phrases.

Certainly, melody and harmony are not the only elements in music. You must also play with expression, nuance, and rhythmical variety. This is to say nothing about charisma and individuality. Despite this, this chapter will focus primarily on the cohabitation of melody with harmony. In other words, this chapter deals only with chords and scales and the unique way in which they interact.

In the following pages, you will find building blocks for improvisation and song writing through various exercises intended to help you better understand what notes go together and what notes do not. Although this was first discussed in Chapter 5, now you will go deeper into this study by analyzing specific chord voicings, bass notes, and bass lines, as they relate to equally specific scalar movements.

Melodies should not be as freewheeling as solos. In contrast, they should be structured to include obvious rhythmical and intervallic repetition. Further, melodic phrases should flow gently into one another, and melodic variations should avoid sudden or abrupt shifts. Rule of thumb: You should be able to hum a melody. If you can't, it's too complex.

Each of the following section headings begins with the word *soloing*. However, the material presented here can also be used to develop melodies for songs. Often, songwriters and composers begin a new tune by noodling at the piano. *Noodling* means that they improvise, experiment, or simply "play around" with intervallic jumps and scalar passages until their ear picks up something they like. Once they hear a snippet of music that they think has potential, they begin fashioning it into a melody replete with chords and a bass line.

Good songwriters know the difference between tunes that are quality and tunes that are lackluster. You may be thinking, "But music is subjective, isn't it?" The answer is yes. However, it is only subjective to a point. Often, song quality is judged by the merits of the melody. Chord changes can always be adjusted or tailored to fit the melody better. However, melodies are the selling points of a tune. If a song has a poor melody, it will quickly fall into obscurity or it may not even be heard.

While this chapter focuses on modal soloing, it will perhaps open the floodgates for song writing. As you move through this book, think about how notes (scales and chords) relate to one another. Also, think about how chord voicings fit with melodies. Voicings are a critical component since they emphasize certain notes and intervals and avoid others. For detailed information on this topic, see Chapter 12.

Soloing with the Harmonic Minor Scale

As you know from Chapters 4 and 5, both the harmonic minor and the Dorian mode contain minor thirds. Yet, they differ on the sixth and seventh scale degrees. The harmonic minor uses a minor sixth interval and a major seventh interval. The Dorian mode uses a major sixth interval and a minor seventh interval. So while these scales are cousins, they are by no means the same. Therefore, be sure not to confuse them!

The harmonic minor scale was chosen for further discussion in this chapter because it is very useful when you wish to evoke an exotic or "foreign" feel to your music. This is especially useful in progressive rock or art-rock styles. First, try playing the scale tones using a basic triad. **FIGURE 8-1** shows this in the key of A minor. The harmonic minor fits perfectly over a minor i chord in different inversions.

Now solo over i, iv, and V chords. The result should be an interesting modal exploration that hints at baroque and classical music. Why? These

FIGURE 8-1: Using the Harmonic Minor Scale

TRACK 17

styles of European classical are very diatonic. Unlike the mid to late romantic period, baroque and classical remain attached to tonal centers. It wasn't until composers such as Frederick Chopin (1810–1849) and Franz Liszt (1811–1886) came along that piano harmony began to embrace deep chromaticism, unexpected key modulations, and dissonant harmonic extensions.

FIGURE 8-2 shows one possible harmonic minor improvisation over i, iv, and V chords.

Using Arpeggios

Look again at **FIGURE 8-2**. On beat three of measure five, you will see the notes G#, B, D, and F. Alone, this outlines a diminished seven chord. However, given that there is an E in the bass, these notes really outline an E7 flat 9 chord. Rather than thinking of this passage as an outline, think of it as a broken chord. In musician's parlance, this is called an arpeggio.

Arpeggios allow pianists to play chords in a more spread-out fashion. Often, they can be used to ornament the music while maintaining the purity of the chord progression. When playing an arpeggio, you do not hit every chord tone simultaneously. Instead, you strike each tone separately as you travel up or down the keyboard.

When played very fast, arpeggios sound like rolls up or down the keyboard. The most common way to "roll" a chord is from the lowest pitch to the highest pitch. This is notated using an arpeggio symbol, which looks like this: {. On occasion, a songwriter asks you to roll a chord from the top pitch to the bottom pitch. In this case, a downward arrow is attached to the arpeggio symbol signifying a descending roll. The arpeggio symbol is not used in this book, but you will see it in sheet music so you should know what it looks like and what it means.

FIGURE 8-2: Using the Harmonic Minor over i, iv, and V Chords

TRACK 18

When playing arpeggios, pianists will often depress the sustain pedal. By doing this, you can better connect the notes of the chord. When you connect notes, you are playing legato. Legato allows notes to flow seamlessly into one another. However, in some contexts, you may not want to play legato arpeggios. In contrast, you may want chord tones to be detached or staccato. When arpeggios are staccato, they can be used as a melodic device. J. S. Bach was the master of this. If you return to the arpeggio in

FIGURE 8-2, you will see that the E7 flat 9 chord described earlier takes on a melodic role since it is played in a detached fashion.

Arpeggios allow chords to "open up" or "breathe." They have often been described as harplike since they really make chords sparkle. Moreover, when you play arpeggios, your chords will sound denser and thicker. Executed properly, arpeggios can add expression and excitement to your music.

Look at a basic minor i chord arpeggio in **FIGURE 8-3**. You will see that scale degrees one, three, and five are used to create a broken A minor chord. Feel free to add pedaling for a fuller effect. When you do this, depress the pedal before you strike the first note and hold it down for the duration of the arpeggio. Since you're playing all chord tones, the pedal will not make this arpeggio sound muddy or incoherent.

FIGURE 8-3:

Minor Arpeggio

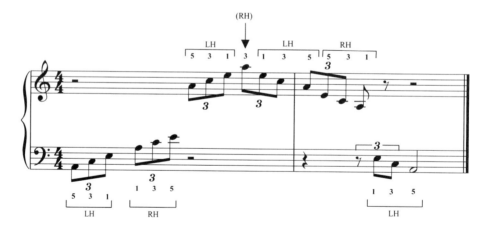

Be very careful of the fingering in this exercise. It is indicated in brackets. You may also play major arpeggios. **FIGURE 8-4** shows the same pattern as **FIGURE 8-3** but with one very important distinction. The difference lies in the use of major thirds not minor thirds. In other words, this figure is played in A major not A minor. Unlike A minor, A major has three sharps: F-sharp, C-sharp, and G-sharp.

FIGURE 8-4:
Major Arpeggio

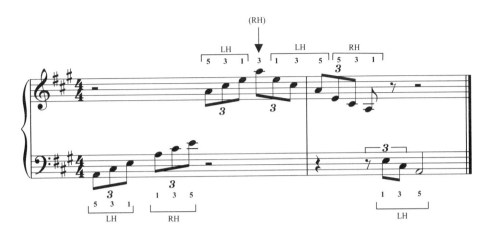

As you might have guessed, you can turn any chord type into an arpeggio. Diminished, half diminished, augmented, major sevenths, minor nines can all be turned into an arpeggio. Think about how you might use arpeggios to add sugar and spice to your own songs.

Soloing with the Dorian Mode

The Dorian mode is a fun improvisational tool. In rock, it's great for one-chord jams. For example, if you're grooving out on a D minor seven, a D Dorian scale is perfect for soloing. **FIGURE 8-5** shows some simple scalar explorations with the Dorian mode. When a D minor triad is paired with the D Dorian mode, you can't go wrong. In fact, this chord is "best friends" with the D Dorian mode. Various D minor inversions are used in this example to show you the simpatico between this scale and this chord.

When playing a melody over inverted chords, make sure that your hands don't collide. Often, novices find that their right hand is moving down the

FIGURE 8-5:
Using the
Dorian Mode

keyboard just as their left hand is traveling up the keyboard. The result is a tangled mess. The best way to avoid this is to be prepared to drop your left hand down to play bass notes when your right hand descends into the third and fourth octave ranges of the piano.

Next, try something a little more musical. **FIGURE 8-6** uses both arpeggios and other melodic devices to create a miniature D minor jam using the D Dorian mode.

FIGURE 8-6: D Minor Jam Using Dorian Mode

TRACK 19

In this example, arpeggios are used on measures one, four, and, to a lesser degree, six. On these measures, you are playing tonic, mediant, and dominant intervals also known as scale degrees one, three, and five. As you learned in Chapter 6, in the key of D minor, scale degrees one, three, and five outline a D minor triad (D, F, and A).

In **FIGURE 8-6**, all of the other notes played in the right hand center around a D minor chord with extensions. For example, in measure five, a major nine interval (E) is stressed. Major nines always spice up minor chords nicely. Be careful when playing the left hand bass pattern on measures five through eight. You will want to play those perfect fifth intervals (D and A) softly and detached. Try your own improvisations using the D Dorian mode. It's an easy mode to manipulate since it uses only white keys.

Pianists generally play chords in their left hand and melodies or solos in their right hand. However, you don't always need to play this way. Switch it up by playing chords in your right hand while soloing in your left. This will help you develop equality between your hands. It will also encourage you to integrate your hands and fingers.

Soloing with Major and Minor Pentatonics

Pentatonics fit well over both major and minor chords. For example, try using them over a major I chord vamp. What's a vamp? A vamp is a section in a piece of music that repeats on loop. Like this example, it often comprises only one chord.

Sometimes, vamps occur at the end of a piece. Other times, they are interludes or breaks in the action. Further, vamps can be used to bridge the gap between the end of one song and the beginning of another. For example, a vamp may be used to segue from one song to the next.

In popular music, pianists often improvise over vamps. Since vamps usually contain a static harmonic progression, pentatonics are a good choice for soloing. **FIGURE 8-7** shows you an example of a vamp in C major. Notice how suspended four (sus4) chords are used in measures six through nine. Also, don't forget to add the pedaling on measure five.

As you know, pentatonics can also be used in minor keys. **FIGURE 8-8** uses minor pentatonics over a minor i chord. In this case, the minor i chord is a C minor. Here, the right hand plays a repetitive motif that uses the notes B-flat, G, F, E-flat, and C. The left hand only plays C and G, which

FIGURE 8-7: C Major Vamp Using Pentatonics

TRACK 20

are perfect fifths. Without the presence of a major or minor third in the bass, you might be confused about the key and the chord quality. However, a third in the bass would not only sound muddy, it would be superfluous. The right hand firmly plants this music in a minor key given its use of minor pentatonics, particularly the note E-flat. As a result, the left hand chords are free to play shell voicings. The perfect fifth interval in the bass also adds power to the music.

Later on, if you wish, you can fashion this lick into a minor blues. Once you learn the chords and structure of a blues, you can try this lick over the entire form.

FIGURE 8-8:

C Minor Pentatonics over i Chord

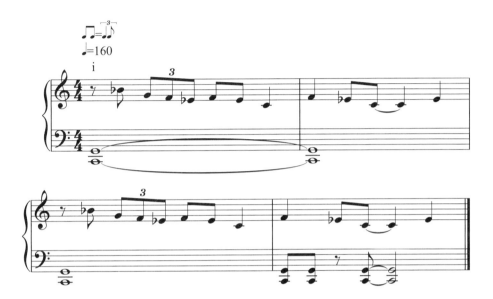

Don't forget to use pentatonics in rock! They are arguably the most widely used scale in this style of music. For example, rock keyboardists might play a repeating major pentatonic over diatonic chord changes. Often, these chord changes consist only of root and fifths (power chords). This is shown in **FIGURE 8-9**.

The kind of repeating phrase used in **FIGURE 8-9** tends to excite audiences who are often wowed by speed and mesmerized by repetition. For better or worse, flashy solos are part and parcel of modern rock. Fortunately, repeating pentatonics like the ones written in **FIGURE 8-9** are easier to play than they sound (and look). Be careful of the dramatic octave ending in this figure. Go slowly on the last two measures and be sure to play each pair of notes cleanly and articulately.

FIGURE 8-9: Major Pentatonics in Rock

Soloing with Blues Scales

As you can imagine, blues scales are the meat and potatoes of blues improvisation. However, they still must be used in a logical, commonsense fashion. You do not want to just simply run blues scales up and down the keyboard. If you do, your playing will sound mechanical and sophomoric.

FIGURE 8-10 is a jazzy blues riff that uses only the notes found in a basic blues scale. In the last two measures, a tri-tone is used between C and G-flat. This tri-tone outlines a C9(flat5) chord, which would be used by players

FIGURE 8-10: Using the Basic Blues Scale

TRACK 22

such as Duke Ellington, Thelonious Monk, and a cornucopia of other jazz-blues pianists. With the proper phrasing and intervallic jumps, this simple blues scale quickly comes alive, hinting at the chic "uptown" riffs used by Harlem pianists in the late 1940s and beyond.

ALERT!

Blues scales are discussed here only in brief, so be sure to see later chapters, particularly Chapter 10, to learn more about blues scale applications. Also, don't hesitate to review Chapter 5 for information on the full, more comprehensive blues scale.

As you can imagine, blues scales invoke the essence and flavors of the blues in ways no other scale can. Therefore, you will want to use them generously. However, don't restrict them only to blues music. Blues scales have wide applications in modern rock and pop. For example, if you listen to rock pianists Keith Emerson (ELP) and John Lord (Deep Purple) or pop pianists Billy Joel and Joe Jackson, you will hear blues scales used constantly.

Soloing with Dominant and Lydian Dominant Scales

The dominant scale is used mostly in jazz blues. But it needn't be! Get creative! There's really no reason to think of scales and chords always in terms of genres. These days, anything is game, and you will hear rock and pop artists combining just about every style of music under the sun.

FIGURE 8-11 shows you one way to use a dominant scale with added chromatics on upbeats. In this example, the dominant scale is used over a I7 chord in C major. That means you're soloing over a C7 chord. Notice how many chromatics are "hiding" in between the diatonic pitches.

If you combine this scale with a blues scale, you have the beginnings of jazz phrases. **FIGURE 8-12** shows you how you might do this. The first half of this four-bar phrase is based on a dominant scale. However, the second half falls squarely into blues scale territory.

FIGURE 8-11: Using a Dominant Scale on a I Chord

TRACK 23

FIGURE 8-12: Bluesy Dominant Scale

TRACK 24

The dominant scale uses a lot of the same notes as the full blues scale. However, the dominant scale tends to fall back on chromatic movement while the blues scale encourages slightly larger intervallic leaps. Both chromatics and intervallic jumps are important. Therefore, combine these scales so that your solos contain variety.

The last scale discussed here is the Lydian dominant. As discussed in Chapter 5, this scale is the same as a dominant scale but with a raised fourth. Often, this raised fourth is called a sharp eleven. **FIGURE 8-13** shows one example of the Lydian dominant set against a I chord.

In this example, when you play F-sharps, you're invoking the Lydian element. Ultimately, the raised fourth adds a harmonic twist to the dominant scale. It also encourages snaky intervallic leaps.

One final note: Be sure to take note of the two arpeggios used in this **FIGURE 8-13**. The first arpeggio occurs on beats three and four of the second measure. The notes E, G, B-flat, and D outline a C9 chord. The second arpeggio occurs on measures four and five of the figure. The second arpeggio outlines a simple C7 chord, and it acts as an ornate musical closure.

FIGURE 8-13: Using a Lydian Dominant Scale on a I Chord

TRACK 25

Chapter 9
Elements of the Blues

Now that you understand scales, chords, arpeggios, and rhythms, it's time to make some music. In this chapter, you will use primarily harmony and rhythm to create a basic blues. Later, you will learn about the deep cultural and regional roots that inform this music together with hot licks in the right hand. First, you need to understand the chordal and structural elements that make up the blues.

I–IV–V *Chord Progressions*

Reduced to its simplest form, the blues comprises three chords. Using roman numerals, these chords are I (tonic), IV (subdominant), and V (dominant). Remember that the I chord or tonic is always your home base. What is the significance of the I chord in the blues?

- All chords eventually resolve to a I chord.
- Songs always begin with a I chord.
- Songs almost always end with a I chord.
- The I chord defines the key. For example, if the I chord is C, the key of the music is C major. If the I chord is a B-flat minor, the key of the music is B-flat minor.

FIGURE 9-1 is a review of the I, IV, and V chords in root position. (If you're reading chapters out of order, it's a good idea to go back to Chapter 6 to review the diatonic triads.) Like most of the examples in this book, the I, IV, and V chords in **FIGURE 9-1** are written in C major.

FIGURE 9-1: I, IV, V Chords in Root Position

C Major   F Major   G Major

You were first introduced to these triads in Chapter 6. However, these chords were only applied as musical snippets. In this chapter, you will learn how to make music with these chords by playing over a twelve-bar blues.

FACT

A chorus is not just a vocal group. It is a musical term that means "the form" or "the structure" in music. A chorus is a musical loop. All choruses contain a strict number of bars as well as a harmonic outline. Choruses may contain any number of bars. The twelve-bar blues is a very popular type of chorus.

In **FIGURE 9-2**, the I, IV, and V chords have now been altered to fit nicely under your fingertips in the right hand (treble clef). The I chord remains unchanged. However, the IV chord is now changed to second position. This means that the "C" or fifth interval of the chord is placed the bottom. The V has also been changed to first position. This means that the "B" or third interval of the chord is placed on the bottom. Notice that the D or fifth interval of the chord has been left out. Because fifths are consonant, they have little harmonic value. In this case, the fifth has become an expendable note. Last, a flatted or dominant seventh (blue note) has been added to the V chord. This is the "F" seen on the first space of the staff. Be sure to note the fingerings.

FIGURE 9-2:
I, IV, V Chords
Voiced for the
Right Hand

These chords can also be played in the left hand, although in blues piano, the left hand is usually reserved for bass lines. **FIGURE 9-3** shows a I–IV–V chord progression written on the bass clef. As you may have guessed, the chords are written in a lower octave. Other than the placement on the

FIGURE 9-3:
I, IV, V Chords
Voiced for the
Left Hand

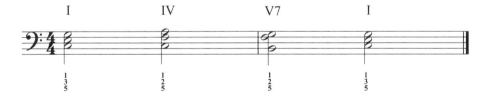

keyboard, the notes in this figure are identical to those used in **FIGURE 9-2**. Again, be sure to use the correct fingerings.

Twelve-Bar Blues

If you read nothing else in this book, be sure to read this section. You cannot and will not understand the blues until you learn the twelve-bar form. This form is ubiquitous. From Muscle Shoals to New York, London to Lubbock, you'll find musicians everywhere using this form. Jazz musicians, folk singers, country yodelers, delta blues raconteurs, oldies rock-n-rollers, swing bands, gospel choirs, heavy metal bands, and many, many others use the twelve-bar blues in their music. In fact, it is the most widespread and universally recognized chord progression in popular music. Thousands of songs use this form, and more and more are being penned every day.

If a chord is major, the music might simply say C, F, or G, for example. You needn't write out the word *major*, although some publishers choose to include the abbreviation *maj* or *ma*. Others may use an upper-case M or a small triangle after the letter name. The triangle is not as universally known, so unless you're writing jazz music, it's best to avoid the triangle.

It's time to look at the twelve-bar blues in detail. Do you remember from Chapter 6 the two cadences that are formed when you couple a I chord with either a IV or a V chord? When you pair it up with a IV chord, you have a plagal or "amen" cadence (I–IV–I). When you pair it up with a V chord, you have an authentic cadence (I–V–I). These cadences are used very effectively in the blues. In **FIGURE 9-4**, you will see the chord symbols for a standard twelve-bar blues.

There are actually thirteen measures written in **FIGURE 9-4**, but don't be confused. Think of the thirteenth measure as measure *one* since this measure marks the return to the top of the form. It is included here so that you can see the authentic cadence that exists between the last measure of the form and the first measure of the new chorus.

FIGURE 9-4:
Chord Symbols for
a Twelve-Bar Blues

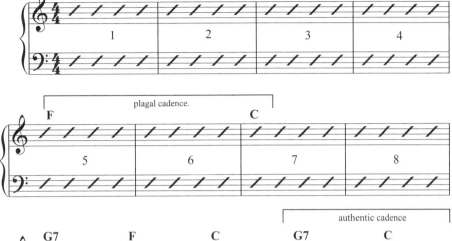

Chord Symbols and Fake Books

In **FIGURE 9-4**, and in examples from previous chapters, you should have noticed chord symbols written above the staff. This is a standardized practice. For example, if you ever play out of a fake book, you will see chord symbols written in this fashion. Fake books are collections of popular songs. They are called fake books because musicians use them to "fake" their way through songs they haven't memorized. Usually the songs are culled from the *Great American Songbook* and feature works by Irving Berlin, George Gershwin, Cole Porter, and other classic songsmiths. In a fake book, the song's melody is written out and chord symbols outline the harmony. It's up to the performer to interpret or "voice" these chords properly.

Hash Marks in Notation

You will also notice that in **FIGURE 9-4** hash marks (/ / / /) were used on the staff. This is because the example did not use any actual notes. For the most part, hash marks tell you that you're free to comp as you wish. *Comp*, or *comping*, refers to the harmonic and rhythmical accompaniment. If a pianist is playing with a singer, for example, he or she will comp chords in order to support the melody. Music is often thought of in layers. If you look at music this way, you could say that comping exists beneath the melody. The melody is the loudest element in a song. The comping or harmonic content is the softer underpinning. This applies to band situations and to solo instrumental situations. On the piano, if you're playing chords and a melody, make sure that the melody sings out over the harmony.

Basic Blues

In **FIGURE 9-5**, you will see a basic blues written out note-for-note. This blues has little application in the real world. No blues pianist would actually play a blues that is this bare. However, for educational purposes, it's good to see the blues stripped down to its parts. Notice that the form is laid out for you in four-bar phrases. Think of the twelve-bar structure in three groups of four measures: 4 + 4 + 4 = 12.

In a twelve-bar form, the I chord is played for four measures. This is followed by two measures of the IV chord. Next, you return to the I chord for two measures. In the last four-bar phrase, there is more harmonic movement. Measure nine features the V (or V7) chord, followed by one measure of the IV chord. Moving to the IV chord is optional. For example, some early boogie-woogie pianists used to hang on the V chord for two bars. Measure eleven returns to the I chord, and finally, measure twelve is another V chord. Moving to the V chord on the last measure is also optional. Sometimes, pianists will stay on the I chord for measures eleven and twelve. However, for this figure, the twelfth measure does move to a V7 chord, creating an authentic cadence with measure I on the repeat.

The repeat sign is found at the end of the music. It is made up of a thick black line, a skinnier black line, and two dots in each clef.

FIGURE 9-5: A
Basic Blues

The Left Hand

Some would argue that the left hand is the most important element in blues and early rock. **FIGURE 9-5** used only quarter notes in the left hand. Although this is a good starting point, it is ultimately too bland. Blues piano is often marked by fancy left-hand work particularly if you play in the boogie-woogie or stride-piano styles. When the left hand is active, the music has greater drive and forward momentum. It is more exciting and exhilarating to listen to. Some blues also contains themes of traveling down the road or riding on rail cars. An active left hand complements such themes by giving the music a locomotive feel.

You should familiarize yourself with a whole host of left-hand patterns. This book only outlines the most popular and common patterns used in blues. However, there are others, and you can also make up your own!

FIGURE 9-6 shows you a simple left-hand pattern that can (and should) be used often. This pattern moves from the I to the IV chord with each beat. Although the chords are changing a lot, harmonically this pattern is really an embellishment on the I chord. Notice that only two notes appear in each chord. You do not always have to play triads or four-note chords. In fact, it's common to play chords with certain chord tones missing; these are called shell voicings. When you play a shell voicing, you omit certain notes. Depending on the context, they can be virtually any note, although they are usually consonant tones. In this figure, you are playing the root and fifth on the I or C chord and an inverted fifth and third for the IV of F chord. The C remains a constant throughout, giving the pattern a I chord feel. In the real world, this pattern is used mainly for fast tempos (speeds). Be sure to note the fingering, which is indicated under the notes.

Don't forget to listen to the masters of boogie-woogie. Check out the music of Willie "Pinetop" Perkins, Pete Johnson, Albert Ammons, Meade "Lux" Lewis, and Charles "Cow Cow" Davenport. These pianists invented and codified the left-hand blues patterns that musicians use today. If you want to play the blues, know its history and roots.

The Shuffle

In Chapter 3, you learned about swing eighth notes. Swing eighth notes are at the root of the shuffle. It's hard to say where the musical term *shuffle* came from. However, it is common in blues and rock, and you may very well hear musicians using this term on the bandstand.

FIGURE 9-6:
Beginner Left-
Hand Bass Pattern

As stated in Chapter 3, swing eighth notes are really triplets. In **FIGURE 9-7**, you will see two notation examples of the shuffle rhythm. In the first measure, the shuffle is represented by triplets. This is literally how swing eighth notes (or shuffle eighth notes) are to be interpreted. The goal is to invoke the long-short feel of this rhythm.

The shuffle can be traced all the way back to the first quarter of the twentieth century with barrelhouse piano styles. Other examples include Delta blues guitarist Johnnie Temple's "Lead Pencil Blues" (1935) and Bob and Earl's "Harlem Shuffle" (1963). The latter was dusted off and rerecorded by the Rolling Stones in 1987.

In the second measure of **FIGURE 9-7**, you will see a dotted eighth-sixteenth rhythm that is also commonly used to denote shuffles. However, this rhythm ultimately breaks down into four sixteenth notes, so it does not accurately represent the shuffle. Remember, the shuffle must always have a long-short triplet feel. For the purposes of this book, shuffle rhythms will always be written as swing eighths. See **FIGURE 3-26** (Chapter 3) for a notational example of swing eighths.

FIGURE 9-7:
Shuffle
Notation

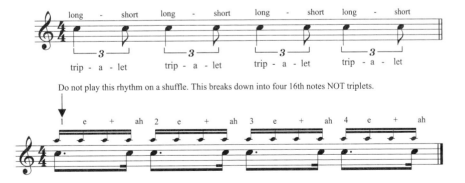

Now it's time to apply shuffle rhythms to the piano. Previously, you learned how to play I–IV chords in succession using quarter notes. In **FIGURE 9-8**, those quarter notes have been changed to swing eighths. This pattern is very common with blues pianists and early rock-n-rollers such as Little Richard and Jerry Lee Lewis. Just like **FIGURE 9-6**, the fingering in the left hand is "one and five" throughout. Notice that your fifth finger (pinky) never moves to a new piano key.

FIGURE 9-8:
Shuffle Pattern
Using I–IV Chords

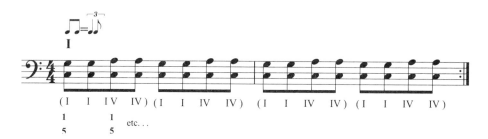

You can take the same shuffle idea and use thirds alternating with the root to create a slightly different feel (See **FIGURE 9-9**). This is also a very effective way to use I and IV chords in rapid succession. Again, the fifth finger (pinky) remains stationary. However, for this pattern, you will need to use your second and third fingers alternately.

FIGURE 9-9:
Shuffle Pattern
Using Staggered
Thirds

Boogie-Woogie

One of the great piano traditions is boogie-woogie. In this book, this style of playing will come up time and time again since its influence is enormous. Boogie had a strong hand in the development of jump blues, country and western, and rock-n-roll. It also greatly influenced the big bands of the swing era including those of Duke Ellington and Tommy Dorsey.

In the first quarter of the twentieth century, boogie was developed in the barrelhouses or rural shanties of the American South. There, poor black day laborers began experimenting with an up-tempo style of music that was fun to dance to. Soon boogie-woogie flourished in the honkytonks or rowdy saloons of the southern states. Eventually, black musicians seeking a better life moved north, bringing this style of music to such cities as Chicago and New York. In 1938, pioneers of boogie-woogie were featured in a series of concerts at Carnegie Hall in Manhattan called "From Spirituals to Swing." Because of these concerts, boogie-woogie reached a larger audience. By the 1940s, boogie would become a short-lived but significant national fad.

Boogie-woogie is largely a solo piano style of music. However, it was sometimes played by piano duos and trios. For example, the Meade "Lux" Lewis, Albert Ammons, and Pete Johnson trio was legendary. In the early 1940s, the Andrew Sisters' movie theme "Boogie Woogie Bugle Boy of Company B" typified the boogie craze with white audiences.

Boogie is characterized by an "eight to the bar" left-hand ostinato. An *ostinato* is a repetitive musical figure played as a loop. In boogie-woogie, a fast-paced, pulsating left hand is used to keep the music chugging along. In addition to Meade "Lux" Lewis, Albert Ammons, and Pete Johnson, Jimmy Yancey, Clarence "Pinetop" Smith, and "Cow Cow" Davenport, were also major developers of this blues style.

Since left-hand activity defines this style, you will want to learn some common boogie ostinatos. **FIGURE 9-10** is a basic boogie pattern. Be careful of the fast tempo. Boogies require a certain amount of technical virtuosity. However, never sacrifice clean, articulate playing for speed. Start slowly and gradually increase your velocity. This figure outlines a C or I chord.

Now, try a more complex bass line. See **FIGURE 9-11**. This ostinato utilizes octaves in the lower register of the piano. Again, note the fingerings and tempo; this figure also outlines a C or I chord.

FIGURE 9-10: Boogie-Woogie Bass #1

TRACK 26

FIGURE 9-11: Boogie-Woogie Bass #2

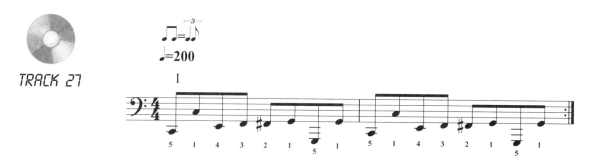

TRACK 27

Walking Bass Lines

Walking bass lines are used very effectively in blues music. For example, you will hear them in boogie-woogie, jump, jazz blues, and modern electric blues. On piano, walking bass lines simulate an acoustic or electric bass player. These days, some jazz combos will omit the bass player altogether. In this situation, keyboardists will often "split" the sounds on their digital pianos, so that the lower register uses a bass sample and the middle and upper registers use a piano sample. (See Chapter 16 for information on equipment and samples.) Needless to say, pianists who play in group settings without a bass player must be proficient with walking bass.

In **FIGURE 9-12**, you see the classic walking bass pattern used in the blues. Notice how the flatted or dominant seventh (blue note) is used on the I, IV, and V chords.

FIGURE 9-12:
Classic Walking
Bass Line

Once you feel comfortable playing the left hand alone, try adding some chords in the right hand. **FIGURE 9-13** shows one way to add some chords. With the exception of the V chord, this figure utilizes triads. If you're feeling adventurous, try adding dominant sevenths to all of the chords.

FIGURE 9-13: Classic Walking Bass Line with Chords Added

TRACK 28

In **FIGURE 9-14**, you will see a variation on the classic walking bass line. This variation simply uses swing eighth notes. In other words, this figure combines the shuffle rhythms learned in **FIGURE 9-8** with a walking bass line.

FIGURE 9-14:
Walking Bass Line
with a Shuffle

Only the I chord is outlined here, but you should be able to easily adapt this rhythm to the IV and V chords. This figure is also similar in feel and style to the boogie-woogie pattern you learned in **FIGURE 9-10**.

Another popular twist on the classic walking bass line includes use of octaves. Octaves will give you a big, rounded sound. For **FIGURE 9-15**, you will use your first and fifth fingers exclusively. Again, try using this idea on a full twelve-bar blues.

FIGURE 9-15:
Walking Bass Line
in Octaves

In jazz blues, pianists will use variations on the blues scale in combination with passing chromatics to create colorful walking bass lines. However, unlike the other patterns learned in this chapter, these walking bass lines are rarely used as ostinatos. Instead, the jazz pianist will continually change or alter the path of the bass line. This keeps it fresh and attention-grabbing.

FIGURE 9-16 is an example of a jazz walking bass pattern. Think of this as a starting point. There are many options to choose from, and you should

FIGURE 9-16: Jazz Blues Bass Line

TRACK 29

try coming up with your own lines. When walking over a blues, remember that passing chromatics must be used on beats two and four only. The strong beats—one and three—must always contain notes from the mixolydian scale (see Chapter 5). One additional warning: When walking, avoid the fourth scale degree or natural eleventh on strong beats; this applies to I, IV, and V chords.

Two-Beat Bass Lines

The two-beat bass line is also used in jazz blues. Dixieland musicians, swing players, big band musicians, and modern jazzers all employ this feel. Stride piano also uses a two-beat feel as the pianist moves alternately from single bass notes to chord voicings (see Chapter 11).

A two-beat feel gives music a happy lift and a light, nimble feel. **FIGURE 9-17** shows the most basic two-beat pattern. Notice that it contains only roots and fifths.

FIGURE 9-17: Basic
Two-Beat Bass Line

While **FIGURE 9-17** is a simple bass line, it is used by pianists at very fast speeds. **FIGURES 9-18** and **9-19** show two other two-beat options. You'll notice that roots and fifths remain the cornerstones of each figure. Everything else that is played is decoration or embellishment.

In the **FIGURE 9-18**, an anticipatory eighth note is included on the *and* of beat four. This is common practice among pianists. Remember to give this a swing feel. If you don't, the pattern will sound Latin.

FIGURE 9-18: Two-
Beat Bass Line with
Anticipation on the
and of Beat Four

Last, **FIGURE 9-19** shows you a two-beat pattern with passing tones. These notes, situated one half step away from either the root or the fifth, simulate a pitch slide. Slides are common in blues music, but since pianists use a fixed keyboard, they can only imitate the slides and pitch bends used by brass and woodwind instruments, singers, and others. You will learn more about "sliding" in Chapter 10.

FIGURE 9-19: Two-
Beat Bass Line with
Passing Tones

Chapter 10
Riffs, Embellishments, Turnarounds, and Endings

Blues piano is full of riffs, embellishments, turnarounds, and endings. In the following two chapters, you will learn some of these tricks of the trade, which include bluesy runs up and down the keyboard, embellishments, and other fancy musical decorations. When used properly, tremolos or rolls, grace notes, glissandos, dynamic shifts, accents, turnarounds, and endings can really make your music come alive. All of the musical examples in this chapter can also be applied to rock music.

Common Riffs

If you're interested in learning the language of blues, you will need to understand the clichés used by virtually all blues players. Not surprisingly, the blues scale is used constantly in this music. If you've forgotten how these scales are played, look back to Chapter 5 to see both the basic blues and the full blues scale. Your job is to use these scales to create melodic lines or riffs. At first, you may find that you play rather mechanically. This is okay. Eventually, you will start to hear some lines forming in your head that actually sound like music. The goal is to develop improvisational spontaneity, which is the very essence of the blues.

The best way to develop your melodic sense is to listen to the blues. In other words, you'll need to steep yourself in the culture of the blues to develop an ear for what is idiomatic and what isn't. This means listening to players from different eras. Don't just listen to New Orleans pianists, Chicago blues men, or British ex-pats. Listen to a smattering of blues artists from all walks of life.

QUESTION?

Who should I be listening to?
Check out Appendix A for a comprehensive list of artists and recordings. There you will find pianists such as Jay McShann, Dr. John, Marcia Ball, Charles Brown, Pinetop Perkins, Thelonious Monk, Duke Ellington, James P. Johnson, Brother Jack McDuff, and many more.

Start off by playing blues scales. **FIGURE 10-1** gives you eight basic riffs to get you going. In these figures, some attempt has been made to create little turns or twists in the direction of the melodic line. These twists make the music more interesting. If you can develop riffs with unexpected intervallic twists, you will be well on your way toward creating what musicians call "snaky" lines. Wherever the line travels, make sure you play only notes within the blues scale(s) in combination with chromatic passing tones. The important thing is to end your lines properly.

If you're playing over a C7 chord, you should end your line on C, G, B-flat, or, possibly and only on occasion, G-flat. There are other possibilities,

FIGURE 10-1: Basic Blues Riffs

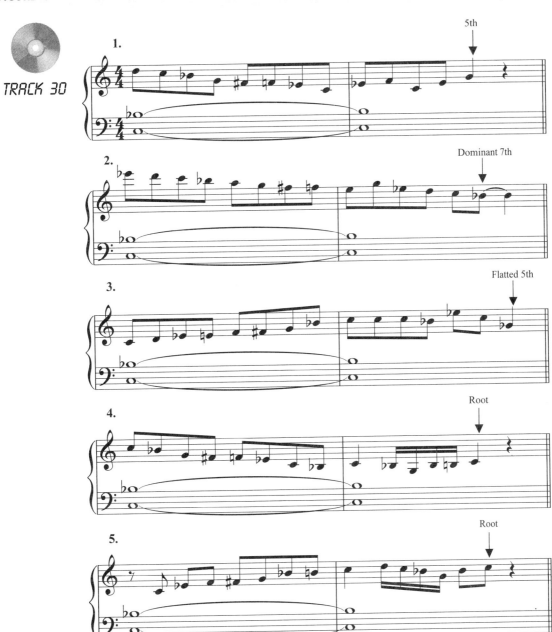

TRACK 30

FIGURE 10-1 (continued): Basic Blues Riffs

but these are the most obvious note choices for beginners. Be sure to listen to the CD to better understand the triplet pattern used in pattern number seven. Switching from eighth to sixteenth note triplets can be a little confusing. Remember that sixteenth note triplets are exactly twice the speed as their eighth note counterparts.

Call and Response Phrases

Now that you're moving your hands around the keyboard and experimenting with blues scales, try creating some call and response phrases. In **FIGURE 10-2**, you will see one possibility. This is a four-bar phrase divided into two equal mini-phrases. In this case, the "call" occurs in the treble clef while the "response" occurs in the bass. Call and response is very common among musicians who sing while they play. For example, a pianist might sing a couplet and then respond with a run down the keyboard. Among others, Ray Charles was fond of doing this. Call and response can also be used between two or more musicians; this is usually referred to as trading licks. In **FIGURE 10-2**, you will play a call and response phrase between your two hands.

FIGURE 10-2: Call and Response Phrase

TRACK 31

Musicians—blues and otherwise—have long used the analogy of storytelling to explain the process of making music. In order to tell an interesting and convincing story, you will need to communicate clear, easy-to-understand musical sentences. This is why phrasing is so important. Phrases are your most important building blocks. Only through careful phrasing can you transform notes and riffs into a musical story. In the end, the quality of your story depends, in large part, on the quality of your phrases.

In blues, phrase lengths can vary greatly. Phrases can be as short as two beats or stretched out over the span of an entire chorus. Phrase durations are totally up to you. Just remember that consistency, flow, repetition, climax, and resolution are all important factors to consider when creating phrases.

Repetition

Repetition is one of the hallmarks of blues music. Repetition refers to the reoccurrence or reappearance of musical ideas. Since the blues itself is a repetitive twelve-bar loop, it stands to reason that your musical sentences can also repeat and paraphrase themselves. Duke Ellington's brilliant yet sparse "C Jam Blues" is a perfect example. This little tune uses only two notes—C and G—in the melody. The rhythm is as shown in **FIGURE 10-3**.

FIGURE 10-3: C
Jam Blues Four-Bar
Phrase

This melody is a four-bar phrase. Moreover, it is repeated three times. As you know, $3 \times 4 = 12$. Twelve is the exact number of bars in a blues. You really can't get any more austere than "C Jam Blues" and still play a melody of any substance.

FIGURE 10-4 shows you another repetitive melodic phrase. The chord changes are purposely left out of this example. Use your ear—together with your knowledge of the blues—to add your own left-hand chord voicings. If you're feeling adventurous, try dropping the roots out of each chord. You might want to use major thirds and dominant sevenths as shell voicings.

FIGURE 10-4: Repetitive Right-Hand Riff

TRACK 32

Dynamics and Accents

Dynamics and accents are used in music to give it depth and texture. When you talk, you accent certain syllables, words, and even phrases. The same is true of music. Musicians regularly use dynamics and accents as a way to invoke expression and greater eloquence in their musical phrases. Without these devices, music can sound static and anticlimactic.

FIGURE 10-5 contains an excerpt from a blues with both regular and marcato accents. The sixteenth note triplets (found in the pickup bar and in the third measure) sound like quick rolls up the keyboard. The little dots written above (in some cases below) the note heads tell you to play short, abrupt notes. To do this, lift your fingertips off the piano keys immediately after you strike a note. Short, disconnected notes are called staccato.

Pianists such as Thelonious Monk, Ray Charles, and Mary Lou Williams used strong accents or musical jabs to create depth and excitement in their music. Regular accents look like ➤. Extra-strong or forceful accents are called marcato accents, and they look like ∧.

FIGURE 10-5: Using Accents

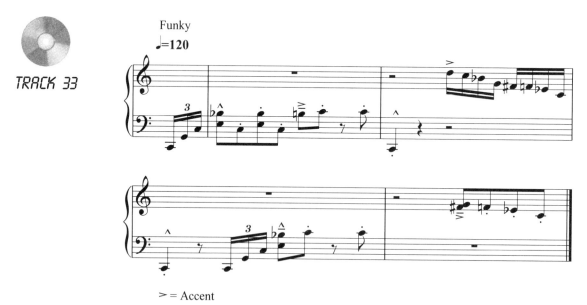

TRACK 33

> = Accent
∧ = Hard Accent (Marcato)

The dashes written above or below a note head tell you to hold out or sustain a note for its full duration; these are called tenuto markings. When playing tenuto, it's okay to press into the keys a little harder than you normally would. For marcato accents, put your entire forearm into it. This will give you that extra strength you need to make those notes really pop out.

Dynamics refer to the volume of the music. Music notation uses the following symbols to indicate volume. The following list moves from softest to loudest:

- *ppp*: Pianississimo, very, very soft (softest)
- *pp*: Pianissimo, very soft
- *p*: Piano, soft
- *mp*: Mezzo piano, medium soft
- *mf*: Mezzo forte, medium loud
- *f*: Forte, loud
- *ff*: Fortissimo, very loud
- *fff*: Fortississimo, very, very loud (loudest)

Crescendos tell musicians to gradually get louder, and decrescendos (also called diminuendos) tell musicians to gradually get softer. In **FIGURE 10-6**, you will see a crescendo and a decrescendo indicated by hairpin-shaped symbols underneath the staff. In this figure, the dynamic shifts from very soft to very loud and then back to very soft. This type of contrast can add intensity to music. Think of this figure as "tension and release." The crescendo represents the building of tension while the decrescendo represents the gradual release of tension. Since dynamics are relative, you must choose how loud or how soft to play each marking. Just remember that contrast is important if you are going to make the dynamics stand out and arc properly.

Embellishments and Decorations

Blues musicians use many embellishments and decorations on notes. Rarely do they play a phrase without at least one embellishment. The best

FIGURE 10-6:
Dynamic Contrasts

way to understand this is through the music itself. **FIGURE 10-7** contains four quarter notes in each measure. The first measure is unadorned, but the second measure is doctored up with half-step intervals on beats two and four. These intervals give the notes a grittier, even uglier, sound; this dissonance is popular in the blues.

FIGURE 10-7:
Half-Step
Embellishment

You can decorate any note you choose. This is common in jazz blues. **FIGURE 10-8** shows you five standard options for ornamenting the note G. The last two examples displace the G rhythmically, but the resolution and focus remain. Keep your ears open for these decorations when you hear bebop pianists play the blues. Also, make sure you transpose these ornaments so that you have them under your fingertips in all keys. By using simple ornaments like these, you can spice up your playing without breaking a sweat.

FIGURE 10-8:

Decorating
a Note

Grace Notes

Grace notes are a pianist's best friend, and those who play blues, pop, rock, jazz, and other improvised musical styles use them constantly. In Chapter 9, you learned about slides. Since the piano has a fixed keyboard, the pitches cannot be altered. However, you can simulate the pitch bends and whoops that other instrumentalists employ by using grace notes and glissandos. Grace notes allow you to make small "slides" of usually a half or a whole step, and ultimately, they permit you greater expression on the piano.

The technical word for a grace note is an *appoggiatura*. Grace notes are written in small type, and they are always paired with a main note. Grace notes are never counted; they simply augment or beef up the sound of a main note. Main notes are counted notes such as quarter notes, eighth notes, and triplets.

If you can "grab" a grace note when playing a riff, go for it. Blues and rock pianists use them constantly and even unconsciously. To get some additional experience with grace notes, try going back over the previous blues figures to see where you can fit in grace notes. You'll be surprised at how many you can add.

Grace notes are played a split second before the main note. The best way to understand them is to use the language of percussionists. Drummers play a rudiment called a *flam*. Flam is onomatopoeia. To understand what a grace note/main note should sound like say the word *flam* out loud, being sure to say this word using two separate syllables. The *f* is the grace note and the *lam* is the main note. **FIGURE 10-9** shows you what a grace note and a main note look like paired. In this case, the main note is a quarter note.

FIGURE 10-9:
Grace Note and
Main Note

Now try playing grace notes. The following four measures use grace notes generously. In the last example, two consecutive grace notes have been used. You can use up to seven grace notes before a main note, although this is rarely done. Be sure to play the correct fingerings. If you're moving in half steps from a black key to a white key, you will use the same finger. In this case, place your fingertip on the edge of the black key and slide into the desired white key. If you're moving from a white key to a black key or from a white key to another white key, you will need to use two different fingers. In this situation, the second and third fingers work best.

FIGURE 10-10:
Using Grace Notes

Glissandos (gliss.)

Try singing two notes with your voice. Start on a low-pitched note and slide into a higher-pitched note. Think about Ed McMahon's introduction on the *Tonight Show*. He used to say, "Heeeeeeeeere's Johnny!" Or perhaps you've recently been to a baseball game and heard the umpires yell, "Yerrrrrrrrrrr out!" These are glissandos.

Many standard-pitched instruments can create glissandos or pitch slides. For instance, glissandos are popular on the clarinet. Listen to the opening passage of George Gershwin's "Rhapsody in Blue" for a fantastic, and classic, example.

FACT

Jerry Lee Lewis and Little Richard were masters of the rock-n-roll glissando. They regularly used these embellishments to add excitement and animation to their concerts. Sometimes you will hear pianists play glissandos simultaneously in both hands. One hand will go up the keyboard while the other descends. This creates a large cacophonous sound.

There are many ways to play a glissando on the piano. Since this book focuses on rock and blues, you will be taught a less academic approach to the glissando. The following applies to the right hand only:

- When playing an ascending glissando, use the back side of your fingers and scrape them across the white keys.
- When playing a descending glissando, use the back side of your thumb to slide down the white keys.

In rock and blues, glissandos are usually played on the white keys and with the right hand. However, you can also use the technique described on the black keys. Reverse these techniques to play glissandos in the left hand. For example, when playing a descending glissando, use the back side of your fingers to slide down the keyboard.

As you will learn in Chapter 13, rock-n-roll pianist Jerry Lee Lewis played a lot of glissandos to add bravura to his music. His technique was also rather homespun. In the right hand, Lewis would use the back side of his hand to ascend the keyboard and the back side of his thumb to descend the keyboard. These approaches to glissandos are fairly easy to learn. Try them and use what works best for you. You might also want to watch some live footage of blues pianists so that you can actually see the various techniques that players use; see Appendix B for recommendations.

FIGURE 10-11:
Glissandos

FIGURE 10-11 shows two glissandos in notation. In this example, you will find an ascending glissando and a descending glissando. Be sure to keep the glissandos in time. In this instance, each glissando is worth two beats (half notes). Both of these glissandos are performed with the right hand.

Tremolos

Tremolos or rolls are another kind of embellishment that is used a lot in blues music. They are often used in the right hand alone or both hands together. Rarely do pianists play extended tremolo passages in the left hand alone. Left-hand tremolos are used mostly to play octaves or roots/fifths in the lower register. Chords with thirds, sevenths, and other extensions sound very muddy when played below C3.

Playing tremolos with a consistent and clean roll can be difficult. It is a technique that does require some practice. One of the biggest mistakes pianists make is playing rolls that have no rhythmical foundation. Remember that when you're playing a tremolo, you're really playing a rhythm. The more accurately you play that rhythm, the cleaner your roll will sound.

To develop your ability to play even and consistent tremolos, try practicing major and minor scales in octaves. Set a tempo, and move up and down the keyboard on downbeats. Use your first and fifth fingers for each tremolo. It is best to practice each hand individually; then put them together after you feel confident. Always listen carefully for continuity, smoothness, and evenness.

FIGURE 10-12 shows you two common tremolo rhythms. They are thirty-second notes and sextuplets, respectively. Bear in mind that everything you play is based on tempo. If the speed of a song is fast enough, the tremolo should be reduced to sixteenth notes or eighth note triplets.

FIGURE 10-12:
Anatomy of a
Tremolo

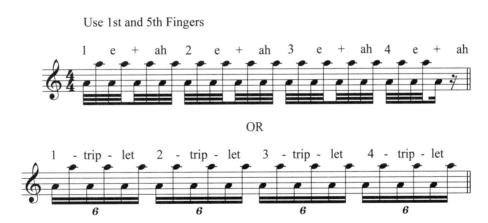

FIGURE 10-13 contains tremolos with various fingerings. After you've learned how to play this figure, try rolling chords that you're familiar with: C7, F, or G7. You should also practice the twelve-bar blues rolling your way through an entire chorus with both hands. Long passages of rolls are common in the

FIGURE 10-13: Tremolos with Various Fingerings

TRACK 34

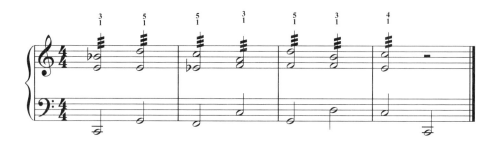

blues. These extended tremolos really make the music build and climax. See Chapter 11, for more information on applying rolls to the blues.

Turnarounds and Endings

Turnarounds and endings are other important blues elements. If you wish to play idiomatically, you will need to add the following figures to your musical toolbox. Like many other styles, the blues has its share of clichés and formulas. It is important to develop your own distinctive voice on the piano. However, you must also play some of the standard moves.

The turnarounds and endings in this book are common. They are used by virtually all blues musicians regardless of whether they come from St. Louis, Sacramento, Austin, Biloxi, or anywhere else on the globe. Mind you, they might not be played exactly note-for-note the same.

A turnaround occurs at the end of a blues chorus. It's a musical signpost that tells the listener, "Okay, we're coming up to the end of a chorus and a new one is about to start." In boogie-woogie, choruses tend to blend into each other without much fanfare. This is because the left hand is chugging away on loop. However, in more lyrical styles of blues, you will often hear pianists use turnarounds to signal the coming of a new chorus. Many turnarounds contain a walking bass line, which moves from the I chord to the V chord. The bass line in **FIGURE 10-14** shows this.

FIGURE 10-14:
Turnaround
Bass Line

Yet, to understand a full turnaround, you'll need to back up to the last phrase of the blues. In **FIGURE 10-15**, a typical bass pattern outlines beginning on measure nine. In this case, the bass line is written using octaves.

FIGURE 10-15:
Four-Bar
Turnaround
Bass Line

FIGURE 10-16 features a full turnaround using both hands. Notice that the third measure (measure eleven in a blues chorus) utilizes the bass line from **FIGURE 10-14**.

The final turnaround uses a ii–V–I chord progression. In Chapter 4, you learned about scale degrees. In the key of C major, a ii chord is minor (D–F–A), a V chord is major (G–B–D), and a I chord is major (C–E–G). This is the harmonic backbone of **FIGURE 10-17**.

Endings are pretty self-explanatory. They are closing licks and/or chord progressions that signal a song's conclusion. There are many well known endings, and you should learn how to play as many of these as possible.

FIGURE 10-16: Four-Bar Turnaround with Both Hands

TRACK 35

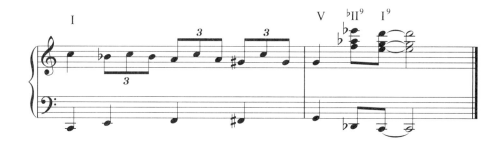

FIGURE 10-17: ii–V–I Turnaround

TRACK 36

FIGURE 10-18: Blues Endings

TRACK 37

Why play stock endings? The blues is built on improvisation, groove, feeling, soul, personal expression, and individualism. However, there are parameters or boundaries. Within those parameters are clichés that everyone uses. You can stretch or deconstruct these musical borders, or simply reinterpret them altogether, but you can't just avoid them. Musical borders are part of the rule book for whatever style of music you are playing. The goal is to strike a balance between originality and convention.

When it comes to endings, the blues almost always favors the clichés. Clever or eccentric endings are rarely used. Soloists may travel outside the usual harmonic boundaries during the body of a song, but the song's ending always brings the music back home to its humble roots.

FIGURE 10-18 features seven stock endings for a major blues. Notice how some of them use the turnaround bass line from **FIGURE 10-14**. Number six is called a tag. It's a rhythmical motif that can be added on to virtually any other ending. Number seven is the standard Basie ending. For more on the inimitable Count Basie, see Chapter 11.

Chapter 11

Blues Across America

The blues is probably best understood through its regional distinctions. In this chapter, you will learn about the similarities and differences between most of these styles. From the Delta to New York City, Chicago to Texas, Memphis to Los Angeles, blues has become an integral part of both rural and urban life in the United States. The blues began in plantations, timber camps, and shantytowns and ended up sweeping across America, giving birth to both jazz and rock-n-roll. This chapter will teach you about the innovators who made it all happen.

Mississippi Delta

As discussed in Chapter 1, the Mississippi Delta is considered the birthplace of the blues. Much of the musical vocabulary that later became integrated into the blues was born in this region. This includes blue notes (flatted third and dominant seventh) and the polyrhythms culled largely from West African music. Further, many of the now-typical lyrical themes of sorrow, heartache, and travel come from the Delta tradition. Plus, the blues as "devil's music" stems from Delta lore.

Writers such as Robert Palmer cite Charley Patton (1891–1934) as a central player in the development of the blues. Some even call him the founding father. Without a doubt, Patton's influence over Son House, Robert Johnson, Howlin' Wolf, John Lee Hooker, and others proves his stature as a blues icon.

While piano was used in the Delta, the classic Delta "sound" is usually defined by solo guitar and voice. The word *Delta* conjures up images of Son House or Robert Johnson in most people's minds. However, boogie-influenced pianists Otis Spann, Sunnyland Slim, and Willie "Pinetop" Perkins were all Mississippians who contributed greatly to the development of the blues in the Deep South. In fact, Perkins was very active in the Delta region during the Depression and the war years as Sonny Boy Williamson's (Rice Miller's) pianist.

FACT

Mississippi-born guitarist and singer Skip James (1902–1969) was also a piano player and organist. James is best known for his open-tuning style of guitar, which musicologists termed the Bentonia School. James had a profound influence on a young Robert Johnson who emulated both James's guitar techniques and his high tenor voice.

FIGURE 11-1 is a tribute to Pinetop Perkins's style. Notice how the right-hand triplets emphasize roots and fifths with a chromatic slide into the first note. Like all boogies, it is best to practice each hand alone since considerable independence is required to perform this music. Also, don't be afraid to use your forearms to really give this boogie some power. There is no such thing as a wimpy boogie.

FIGURE 11-1: Boogie for Pinetop

TRACK 38

Boogie for Pinetop

New Orleans

New Orleans is not just the birthplace of Louis Armstrong. It has long been a hotbed for talented piano players. In fact, there are too many to mention here. Early piano greats include Tony Jackson, Jelly Roll Morton, and Tuts

Washington. Other key players are Champion Jack Dupree, Professor Longhair, Fats Domino, Huey "Piano" Smith, James Booker, Allen Toussaint, and the ever-popular Dr. John (Mac Rebennack). The younger generation boasts Art Neville (The Neville Brothers), Texas transplant Marcia Ball, and the multitalented Harry Connick Jr.

QUESTION?

Did Jelly Roll Morton invent jazz?
He claimed that he did. He had business cards made up that read "Originator of Jazz." Although Morton did not invent jazz, he was a pivotal figure in New Orleans music. His approach to composition reveals both a pioneering spirit and a deep understanding of ragtime, blues, and traditional jazz.

New Orleans piano styles can vary greatly. To this day, many players remain based in boogie-woogie. Others draw from the more sophisticated jazz harmonies. Ellis Marsalis is an example of the latter. Afro-Caribbean rhythms and European folk music from France, Spain, and Portugal also color this music. This is due to the confluence of Cajun and Creole cultures.

In New Orleans, "second-line" snare drum grooves often mingle with tiered brass band melodies. Unlike other blues regions, clarinets, trumpets, trombones, and tubas are clearly favored over electric guitars, harmonicas, and honking saxophones. This gives New Orleans an Old-World charm that no other city can boast. Lastly, the lazy or loping groove used by New Orleans musicians is sometimes given the loose appellation "swamp."

Chicago Blues

The blues came to the Windy City during the 1930s and 1940s when a mass exodus occurred in the Deep South. During this period, Delta musicians headed north in search of job opportunities in factories. Soon the Chicago style of blues was born. In many respects, when people think of the blues they think of the Chicago sound. This is due in large part to the overwhelming popularity of Muddy Waters and Howlin' Wolf, two Delta guitarists/singers who almost singlehandedly defined the new urban sound of the early 1950s.

Waters's bands featured many of the most prominent men in blues including Willie Dixon, Jimmy Rogers, Big Walter Horton, James Cotton, and Junior Wells. He also employed two of the most important blues pianists in history, Otis Spann and Pinetop Perkins, whom you read about earlier in the chapter.

Other significant players on the classic Chicago stage included Buddy Guy, Otis Rush, Sunnyland Slim, and by the 1960s, a young Jewish guitarist named Michael Bloomfield. Many of these artists were recorded by Chess Records.

Chess Records was a legendary blues record label created by Phil and Leonard Chess. Eventually, Chess embraced rock-n-roll, signing Chuck Berry and Bo Diddley in the mid 1950s. In 1969, the brothers sold Chess to General Recorded Tape. Years later, the Music Corporation of America (MCA) purchased the Chess catalog only to be bought out themselves in 2003 by Geffen Records.

The most obvious or salient feature of Chicago blues is the use of electric guitars. This revolutionized the blues and, in some respects, spurned the coming British Invasion. Many British rock bands from the 1960s and 1970s sought to imitate the Chicago blues sound, including the Rolling Stones, the Yardbirds, the Animals (with Alan Price on organ and keyboards), Led Zeppelin, and Deep Purple (with John Lord on keyboards and organ). Today, the Chicago blues scene is still abuzz and the annual Chicago Blues Festival at Grant Park attracts throngs of tourists.

Other Important Blues Regions

Other important blues regions include the Piedmont, Texas, the West Coast, Memphis, St. Louis, Kansas City, and New York City. Each region has a distinct sound and style, along with chief innovators. Piedmont comes from the Piedmont region in the Southeast. Historically, Piedmont blues players were influenced by ragtime and white country fiddle music. However, Piedmont also has strong African roots and cross-pollination continues to take place between the neighboring Piedmont and Delta regions. The Piedmont style is predominantly guitar oriented; its most significant feature is a unique finger-picking technique, which emulates ragtime piano.

Texas blues is more swing and jazz oriented. Singer and guitarist Blind Lemon Jefferson is widely considered the father of this genre, though Lightnin' Hopkins and T-Bone Walker are also synonymous with the Texas sound. Walker's jazzy arrangements often included horn sections and smoky saxophone riffs. His intimate approach also made him something of a sex symbol in the days before television.

In the 1970s and 1980s, Texas also became known for its blues rockers. ZZ Top, the Fabulous Thunderbirds, and the late, great guitar virtuoso Stevie Ray Vaughan all hailed from Texas. If you're looking to hear piano blues from Texas, check out the elegant stride-influenced styles of Rob Cooper and Andy Boy on recordings by the velvety singer Joe Pullum.

West Coast Blues

West Coast blues is the brother to Texas blues. In the late 1940s, many Texans relocated to California, bringing their swing-influenced blues with them. Teenage sensation Little Willie Littlefield was one of them. His early hit "It's Midnight" brought the young pianist great success in Southern California. Charles Brown was another Texan whose smooth-toned ballad singing and jazzy piano style earned him acclaim on the West Coast. The same is true of Floyd Dixon who moved out to the West Coast, eventually replacing Brown in Johnny Moore's popular Three Blazers.

Superstars Nat King Cole and Ray Charles are the pianistic titans of the West Coast, although they were born in Alabama and Georgia, respectively. These men dominated much of the national scene during their heydays. And there is a curious connection between the two. In Clint Eastwood's documentary *Piano Blues*, Charles discusses his obsession with Cole's piano playing. In the film, Charles tells Eastwood that when he was young, he used to eat, drink, and sleep Cole's music. This is evident in early Charles ballads such as "I Wonder Who's Kissing Her Now." As for Cole, he was influenced by the urbane, modern stylings of Earl "Fatha" Hines and the hard-swinging, yet nimble, approach of Count Basie.

St. Louis Blues

St. Louis, Missouri, is also steeped in the blues. Part of this is due to ragtime composer W. C. Handy. Handy never lived in St. Louis, but his song "St. Louis Blues" will always epitomize this central American town. Handy was the first songsmith to prove that the blues had commercial value. Indeed, the composer's tribute to St. Louis demonstrated the power of ragtime and blues music. For a time, no other song could match the enormous popularity of "St. Louis Blues," except perhaps other compositions by Handy himself. This song also transformed a one-time dusty cowboy town into a blues treasure.

FACT

When W. C. Handy first peddled "St. Louis Blues" to publishers, he was turned down flat. He eventually published the song himself in September 1914. Three years later, the bawdy vaudevillian singer Sophie Tucker recorded "St. Louis Blues" to critical acclaim. Her rendition of the song became an instant and massive hit.

Pianist Roosevelt Sykes was another influence on St. Louis blues. His barrelhouse (early boogie-woogie) style made him very popular in St. Louis and throughout the blues circuit. Then there is Peetie Wheatstraw, a transplant whose impact on blues is often overlooked these days, but during the Depression he was extremely popular. Drawing from the work of pianist Leroy Carr and guitarist Scrapper Blackwell, Wheatstraw developed a song-writing style that featured prearranged instrumental introductions and lyrics that appealed to the downtrodden conditions of the working class. Like the Delta blues musicians, Wheatstraw also sought to gain popularity by using tales of the devil to sell his brand of the blues. He even referred to himself as "The Devil's Son-in-Law."

Kansas City Blues

Kansas City was the home of one of the most celebrated boogie-woogie kings, Pete Johnson. Johnson's work with Big Joe Turner helped spawn not only jump blues but also rock-n-roll. Without a doubt, Turner's "Shake, Rattle, and Roll" would go on to galvanize a nation, transforming "race music" into mass-marketed pop music.

Swing was also all the rage in Kansas City during the so-called Golden Age of Jazz (1935–1945). All of the music made in Kansas City during the swing era was blues based, including the work of pianist Jay McShann who successfully combined jazz harmonies with blues and gospel influences.

Jay McShann's orchestra featured a young alto saxophonist named Charlie Parker. Nicknamed "Bird," he went on to become one of the most important saxophonists in history. Along with Dizzy Gillespie, Bud Powell, Max Roach, and a handful of others, Bird created a new, sophisticated brand of jazz called bebop. Despite this, Parker's approach to improvisation was always based on the blues.

For all intents and purposes, the legendary New Jersey pianist Count Basie also got his start in Kansas City during a time of great musical change in America. At the dawn of the swing era, Basie worked with Walter Page's Blue Devils and later with Benny Moten. After Moten's death, Basie formed his own swing orchestra. Over the years, Basie's bands featured many of the finest names in jazz, including saxophonist Lester Young.

Basie lived in Kansas City for only about eight years, but he always stayed true to the Kansas City jump style of swing. This is seen in songs like "One O'Clock Jump" and others. Basie's music was always hard swinging, and his orchestra typically employed great dynamic contrast. They were famous for playing very soft. Then out of nowhere "bam" the drums and horns would really kick in. This was but one of Basie's signatures. On piano, Basie's "less is more" approach set him apart from all the other "chops"-oriented pianists of his time.

Memphis Blues

Memphis blues is largely intertwined with the history of Beale Street. At the turn of the twentieth century, Robert Church paid to have Church Park built on Beale and Fourth. This became an important gathering place for early blues musicians. The legendary ragtime composer W. C. Handy also gave Memphis a shot in the arm by penning two exceedingly famous blues pieces "Memphis Blues" and "Beale Street Blues," published in 1912 and 1916, respectively. During the second quarter of the twentieth century, Beale Street became a cultural melting pot for traveling musicians of all sorts, including various folkies, jug bands, and eventually blues men from the Delta and Chicago. One of those was pianist Sunnyland Slim who played alongside Ma Rainey and Little Brother Montgomery on Beale Street during the Roaring Twenties.

Memphis Slim (no relation to Sunnyland Slim) was a gifted local pianist who also made a name for himself during the early Depression years. A boogie-woogie stylist, Slim eventually moved to Chicago to pursue a record contract and to hook up with the hotshot Delta guys. There he met and played with the legendary guitarist and composer Big Bill Broonzy.

FACT

Guitarist B. B. King got his stage name from performing on the radio in Memphis. For live broadcasts on the progressive station WDIA, Riley King called himself Beale Street Blues Boy. This nom de plume was eventually abridged to Blues Boy and then to B. B.

One riff that has become quite a staple in the postwar Memphis, Chicago, and Detroit blues traditions is shown in **FIGURE 11-2**. This simple triplet pattern is used as a repeating motif. Blues musicians have gotten a lot of mileage out of this lick over the years. One song that uses this pattern is Memphis Slim's "The Comeback." Listen for this riff in the recordings of Muddy Waters, John Lee Hooker, and others.

FIGURE 11-2: Common Blues Motif

TRACK 39

Blues and Jazz in the Big Apple

Blues and jazz in New York City revolve largely around three traditions: swing, stride, and bebop. All of them took hold in upper Manhattan in a predominantly black neighborhood called Harlem. The swing tradition in New York was dominated by Count Basie, Duke Ellington, Benny Goodman, and Chick Webb. Swing became a vehicle for big band arrangements and virtuosic solos, but it was always rooted in the blues. Moreover, it embraced trends such as boogie-woogie and jump.

In the second decade of the century, stride evolved out of ragtime, though some pianists such as Eubie Blake never distinguished between the two styles. The three kings of stride were James P. Johnson, Willie "The Lion" Smith, and Fats Waller. Stride is a very complex style that requires great speed, accuracy, and facility with the left hand. When playing in this style, you play bass notes (usually roots) on beats one and three and chord voicings on beats two and four. While this is going on, the right hand plays a melody, or perhaps, solos overtop. **FIGURE 11-3** shows you a rudimentary pattern using shell voicings and guide tones (thirds and sevenths). Like the previous boogie exercises, this pattern requires some independence between your hands, so practice each hand individually.

Bebop

New York City is also the home of bebop. Contemporary jazz has its roots in bebop, which is a style of jazz that evolved out of the perceived restrictions of the swing era. Swing was ultimately dance music, but around 1945,

FIGURE 11-3: Basic Stride Piano

TRACK 40

instrumentalists began to rebel against the commercialization of jazz. Soon pianists such as Bud Powell and Thelonious Monk began experimenting with extended chord voicings, chromatic flurries, and exotic modalities. Because bebop artists were more concerned with music as art, jazz generally lost its pop and dance appeal. However, the form never lost its blues roots.

Blues progressions were transformed during the bebop period. Instead of playing just I, IV, and V chords, pianists began adding other chordal substitutions to make the blues more harmonically challenging. For example, the modern jazz blues adds ii–V chord progressions, diminished chords, and a complex ending that usually includes a iii–vi–ii–V–I chord progression. Melodically, bop and post-bop musicians also used different modes. One example is the Lydian dominant mode you learned in Chapter 5.

Jazz Blues

The four examples in **FIGURE 11-4** are intermediate blues licks that you can use to spice up your solos without getting too heady or theoretical. The last lick is pretty dissonant, so don't worry about understanding all the melodic twists and turns. Simply listen to the jagged intervallic leaps and take note of the sharp nines and the flatted fifth. In some of these examples, notice how the root (C) is sometimes left out of the accompanying chord. This is idiomatic to jazz. Often, pianists will drop the root, letting the bass player supply it instead.

For the adventure seekers among you, a harmonically complex minor blues has been included in **FIGURE 11-5**. The minor blues is a tradition unto itself, dating all the way back to New Orleans funeral processions. In this figure, you will see ii–V chord substitutions and voicings with stacked thirds. These stacked intervals create harmonic extensions such as sevenths and ninths. Don't worry if you don't understand all the harmonic complexities inherent in this music. Just try this blues and experience the rich chords used throughout. Be careful of the key signature. C minor has three flats (B-flat, E-flat, and A-flat).

Creating Licks with Thirds

Throughout this chapter, you have read about the differences between blues styles. Therefore, it seems fitting to end with some simpler licks that emphasize the similarities between blues genres. The following licks could all be applied to most styles of blues in one way or another. In **FIGURE 11-6**, you will see a series of examples that highlight third intervals. If you don't know what third intervals are, go back to Chapter 4. Like many of the figures used in the previous chapter, these licks build off of the clichés that most blues pianists use on a daily basis.

FIGURE 11-4: Jazzy Right-Hand Riffs

1.

2. Extended Blues scale

3.

4.

FIGURE 11-5: Minor Blues

TRACK 42

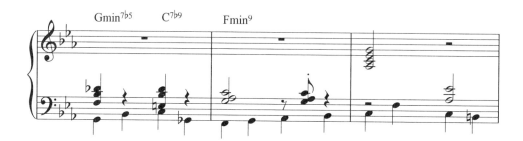

The first example is a simple model of ascending thirds in the right hand only. The second example is more static. Here, half steps are used in the first two measures to decorate the third and fifth scales degrees (E and G). Again, only the right hand is used here.

The next example uses thirds staggered against the root (C), and both hands are integrated. The fourth example also uses staggered third intervals, but this time they are set against the third scale degree (E). This pattern eventually ends on the dominant seventh and fifth. The fifth example uses half and whole steps to descend from B-flat and D (the dominant seventh and ninth) to their counterparts an octave lower. The sixth example returns to staggered third intervals. Like example number three, each pair of thirds is set against the root (C). This pattern also ends on the almighty dominant seventh with an added ninth.

Creating Licks with Sixths

Sixth intervals are very similar to thirds. In fact, they are simply the inverse of a third. For example, if you count up from C six steps, you arrive at A. Similarly, if you count up from A three steps, you arrive at C.

In **FIGURE 11-7**, you will see four examples of licks using sixths. The first pattern ascends from the third and root (E and C) to their counterparts one octave higher. En route, the harmony switches to the IV chord, creating a plagal cadence. The pattern eventually ends on the dominant seventh and fifth. The second example descends from the root and third (C and E) to their counterparts one octave lower. Like the first pattern, this example also utilizes a I–IV progression and ends on a dominant seventh and ninth.

The third example does not use double stops (two notes played simultaneously). Rather, the melody employs intervallic leaps of sixths. Can you count the number of sixth intervals in this pattern? There are a total of five. Like the previous patterns, a I–IV progression is used to allow for more maneuvering with the sixth intervals in the right hand. The last example returns to harmonic intervals or double stops. This pattern ends on the very consonant major third and root. This is done to show that you don't always have to end phrases on blue notes, even when playing the blues.

FIGURE 11-6: Licks Using Thirds

TRACK 43

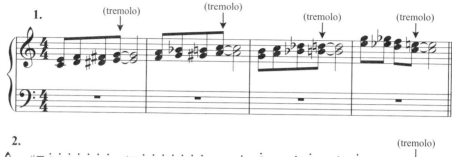

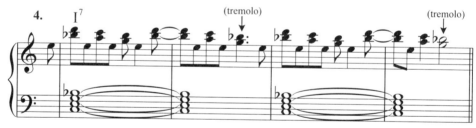

Note: Once you learn each lick, try adding tremolos in the RH where you see (tremolo) written above a pair of notes!

FIGURE 11-6 (continued): Licks Using Thirds

FIGURE 11-7: Licks Using Sixths

TRACK 44

Note: Once you learn each lick, try adding tremolos in the RH where you see (tremolo) written above a pair of notes!

Chapter 12
Elements of Rock

In this chapter, you will learn about the elements that make up rock and pop piano playing. Rock piano mixes earlier traditions and styles freely. For example, the blues, jazz, country and western, rhythm and blues, and European classical all influence what is generically known as "rock" and "pop." Some songwriters even employ Middle Eastern or other ethnic modalities. This chapter will give you some of the necessary tools you will need to begin playing and understanding rock and pop.

Distinguishing Rock from Pop

Rock and pop are similar styles of music; however, the words "rock" and "pop" are problematic since these terms can only be seen through the lens of subjectivity. In other words, these labels mean different things to different people. There is also the matter of preference. Rock is considered noisy and primitive to some listeners. To others, rock is creative, energetic, and exciting. Similarly, some listeners view pop as wimpy, overproduced, and corporate driven. To others, pop is catchy, stylish, and fresh. Still others make no distinction between pop and rock at all; they simply use the terms interchangeably.

In this text, pop will be defined as a milder, streamlined cousin to rock. Pop will be considered more song and hook oriented and less improvisatory. Think of pop as a radio-friendly style of music. This means shorter songs, less jamming, and more emphasis on melody and lyrics. By this definition, artists such as Whitney Houston and Michael Jackson would be considered pop artists. Jimi Hendrix and Led Zeppelin would not since their songs can vary in length and they usually contain lots of improvisation.

Pop is a temporary label used to describe fashionable music of the day. Many symphony orchestras perform "pops" concerts each season. These events offer lighter fare from various eras in musical history. One of the most celebrated pops orchestras is the Boston Pops. This orchestra premiered in 1885 and has been successful ever since.

In this book, rock will be considered more improvisatory and heavy. In other words, it will be more hard edged with less emphasis on nuance. Some artists can be both pop and rock. For example, Paul McCartney wrote the pop tune "Penny Lane" and the raucous rock anthem "Helter Skelter." These are very different song styles, and they show the range of McCartney's songwriting abilities.

Chord Voicings

The good news is that the chord voicings used in rock and pop are basically interchangeable. Both styles pull from the same sources, so you can try applying the musical examples found here to both pop and rock contexts. Most chord voicings in pop and rock are based on triads or inverted triads. Sometimes major sixths, major or minor sevenths, and suspensions are added. Augmented and diminished chords are also used sparingly. If you've forgotten any of these chords, go back and review Chapters 6 and 7.

If you add a lot of harmonic extensions to your music, you will move quickly into the realm of jazz, which may or may not fit with the type of rock/pop you're playing. The music of Steely Dan is the perfect example of pop meets jazz. In their heyday, this group used copious amounts of jazz chords, yet still maintained a pop profile with many radio hits to their credit.

Other pop and rock artists have used intricate chords, too. Notables include Paul Simon, Sting, Simply Red, and, on occasion, Prince. Pianists Stevie Wonder, Joe Jackson, and Bruce Hornsby also regularly use jazzier voicings. Furthermore, earlier progressive rock bands Yes, ELP (Emerson, Lake, and Palmer), and Genesis used greater harmonic complexities, though these were based more on classicism than jazz (see Chapter 14).

Despite the influence of jazz and classical, most rock and pop shies away from harmonic intricacies; some songs may only contain a few basic chords.

The following figure uses staggered chord tones, which is commonplace in both rock and pop. **FIGURE 12-1** shows you a triad broken up between the root and the third/fifth scale degrees of the chord.

FIGURE 12-1:
Staggered Triad

Now add roots in the bass (left hand) and harmonic movement. **FIGURE 12-2** shows you a C major triad moving to a IV chord or F major triad. Notice that the voicing on the F chord is in second position and the note C remains constant on the upbeats.

Voicing really comes down to two rules of thumb:

FIGURE 12-2:
Staggered Triads
Using Both Hands

1. When traveling from chord to chord, choose the least amount of intervallic movement between them.
2. Maintain as many common tones as you can. In other words, if you are moving between two chords and both chords contain the note C, try playing the same C for each chord; don't shift octaves.

This is best illustrated through example. **FIGURE 12-3** shows the cadence V–IV–I. The chords here are voiced in root position. Because these chords are all in root position, the intervallic leap between the IV and I chords is large. This leap should be avoided.

FIGURE 12-3:
V–IV–I in Root
Position

The intervallic leap between the IV and I chords in **FIGURE 12-3** can be avoided by playing an inverted I chord in first position. In **FIGURE 12-4**, you will see how to voice this cadence. Notice how the common tone (C) is maintained on the IV and I chords.

FIGURE 12-4:
V–IV–I Using
Voice Leading

When you use proper voice leading, your music will sound smoother. Voice leading also helps you avoid tricky fingerings, and you won't flub as many notes. In general, thoughtful voice leading will make your playing cleaner, smoother, and more articulate.

Song Forms

There are many song forms used in modern rock and pop but the basic elements are the same for each song. These elements include:

- Introduction
- Verses
- Pre-choruses
- Choruses (or refrains)
- Reintroduction(s)
- Bridge or middle eight
- Solo section(s)
- Outro or coda

There are four other types of songs that may not use these elements.

- Songs built off a riff or single motif (e.g., one-chord jams)
- Songs that are ever evolving and building with no repeated sections
- Stories (usually spoken) set to music
- Songs structured around older forms such as the twelve-bar blues

It would be rare to find any one song that uses all of the elements. A song's design is usually based on the tastes and goals of the songwriter(s). Producers may also influence a song's structure. These days, songs are rarely founded on the Great American Songbook formula which was the basis for hit after hit in the pre-rock era. Great American Songbook tunes often used two sections called A and B. In the 1930s and 1940s, the most common form was AABA and tunesmiths such as Cole Porter, George Gershwin, Hoagie Carmichael, Richard Rodgers, Jerome Kern, Harold Arlen, and others regularly used this song structure.

Structural Elements Defined

An introduction is a short musical prologue or opening passage. Verses tell the story of the song. In most cases, the first verse begins when the lyrics enter. Pre-choruses are optional. They are essentially a supplementary verse structure designed to make the song build seamlessly into the chorus. The chorus contains the hook. Because of this, the chorus or refrain is the most important song element. Often, it is the chorus that sells the song to the listener.

ALERT!

The word *chorus* is used differently in contemporary pop and rock. In these genres, a chorus is the main section of the song where the hook is commonly found. In older traditions, such as blues and jazz, a chorus refers to a complete song form such as a twelve-bar blues or a thirty-two-bar (AABA) bebop or show tune.

When the chorus is sung, you will often hear the song title. If there is a reintroduction, it will be used to loop you back to the beginning of the song. You can bet that after a reintroduction, another verse will follow. A bridge is a sudden shift in the song's mood that often connects a chorus to a third verse or a chorus to another heavier chorus. Key changes are common in bridges, but they are not required. A middle eight is a type of bridge that contains eight measures.

Solo sections sometimes act as bridges. In this case, they give instrumentalists a chance to show off their wares. Solo sections can occur over introduction, verse, or chorus chord progressions. They also may occur over completely new chord changes. Last but not least, outros (the opposite of an intro) and codas are end pieces. Often they mirror the song's introduction, but they can also introduce new musical ideas. Songs with outros and codas often end with a compelling musical twist or a powerful build.

FIGURE 12-5 shows the form to David Bowie's "Changes," a song that features the piano. This song has definite, easy-to-hear parts so it's perfect for analysis. If you don't know this tune, it appears on the album *Hunky Dory* (1971) or the popular compilation *ChangesBowie* (1990). The pianist is Rick Wakeman, whom you will read more about in Chapter 14.

Each section ends with a double bar line and the 2/4 and 3/4 bars are part of the chorus. Listen to the song and count each measure aloud. The best way to count is to say the measure number on beat one of each bar. In other words, count 1, 2, 3, 4 / 2, 2, 3, 4 / 3, 2, 3, 4 / 4, 2, 3, 4, / 5, 2, 3, 4 / 6, 2, 3, 4 and so on.

FIGURE 12-5:

"Changes" Song Structure

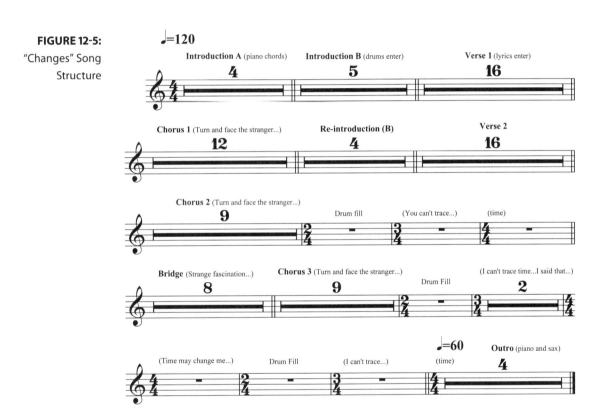

Common Chord Progressions

There are many chord progressions found in pop and rock. In fact, the variations are seemingly limitless. However, there are some standard progressions that songwriters use over and over. The first two examples use only I–IV–V chords. Like the blues, these chords are ubiquitous in rock and pop music. **FIGURE 12-6** shows you I–IV–V changes condensed to an eight-bar phrase (unlike the usual twelve-bar blues). Notice the voice leading in the chords and the passing tones in the bass.

FIGURE 12-6: Eight Bar I–IV–V Progression

TRACK 45

FIGURE **12-7** also uses I–IV–V chord changes. Here, the chords change on each measure, creating a four-bar phrase. Notice how chord inversions are used in each measure to make the music flow easier.

FIGURE 12-7:
Four Bar I–IV–V
Progression

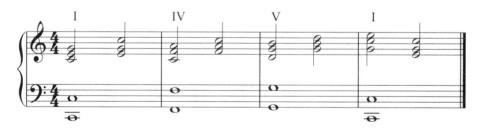

There are many variations available to you using just I–IV–V chords. Try coming up with your own chord progressions using these three chords. You'll be surprised at how many permutations you can create.

Another common chord progression is I–vi–ii–V–I, shown in **FIGURE 12-8**. When you're in a major key like C, the vi and ii chords are minor. Therefore, they are written using lower-case roman numerals (see Chapter 6).

Also, you may substitute the I chord in the beginning of a I–vi–ii–V–I progression with a iii chord. Like the vi and ii chords, a iii chord is minor

FIGURE 12-8:
I–vi–ii–V–I
Progression

in major keys. This changes the voice-leading options and the progression takes on a new color. If you think back to Chapter 6, you will remember that you can also use a deceptive cadence at the end of a phrase. This means that instead of playing the I chord, you can play a vi chord. Try this ending with **FIGURE 12-9**.

Another common progression is I–vi–IV–V–I. **FIGURE 12-10** shows a simple rendering of this. In Chapter 6, you learned that V and diminished vii chords

FIGURE 12-9:
iii–vi–ii–V–vi
Progression

are interchangeable as well. Feel free to make this substitution in the following progression. Finally, if you wish to really change things up, try playing the last chord minor (flatted third). This will take you off in another direction entirely.

Drop-down bass patterns are also common in pop music. In fact, the David Bowie song referenced earlier uses one of these. **FIGURE 12-11** shows one descending bass pattern that you could use. Patterns of this sort often use slashes to separate the chord from the bass note. For example, if you see a C/G that means that you're playing a C major chord with a G in the bass.

The chord progressions in this chapter can all be spiced up with suspended chords as well. If you're comfortable with suspended chords, go back over **FIGURES 12-6** through **12-11** and add suspensions.

FIGURE 12-10: I–vi–IV–V–I Progression

TRACK 46

FIGURE 12-11:
Drop-down Bass
Progression

Spicing It Up with Arpeggios

In Chapter 8, you learned about arpeggios. It's time to put them to work since they are very common in pop and rock. Arpeggios are usually played as eighth notes, sixteenth notes, or triplets. The following chord progression combines I–IV–V chords with sixteenths. The sustain pedal is used to create a beautiful, harp-like effect. In **FIGURE 12-12**, pedaling occurs on each measure. Release the pedal just after you play the last sixteenth note. Then press it down again a millisecond before you play the next bar. Timing is crucial.

FIGURE 12-13 is a similar pattern played as triplets. Notice how chord inversions are used here to make the arpeggios more colorful and melodic.

You can and should come up with your own arpeggios using I–IV–V chords. **FIGURE 12-15** is a more intricate pattern that uses greater harmonic movement. Notice how the IV chord (F major) uses an E in the arpeggio. This is a major seventh. This figure also uses mixed rhythms. You will see a dotted eighth–sixteenth rhythm. To understand this rhythm, picture the beat divided into four parts as illustrated in **FIGURE 12-14**.

The final arpeggio in this chapter employs a left hand crossover. Sometimes pianists play a note that is beyond the reach of the right or left hand. This often happens when playing extended arpeggios. The solution is to

FIGURE 12-12: I–IV–V Arpeggiated

TRACK 47

FIGURE 12-13: I–IV–V Arpeggiated with Triplets

TRACK 48

cross one hand over to strike the note that is out of range. If you're moving up the keyboard, you will cross your left hand over. If you're moving down the keyboard, you will cross your right hand over. **FIGURE 12-16** (see page 182) is a pop progression that uses extended harmonies and hand crossing. Play this figure slowly at first and follow the fingering strictly.

FIGURE 12-14:
Dotted Eighth–
Sixteenth Rhythm

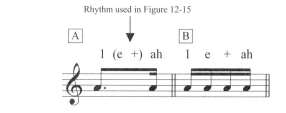

FIGURE 12-15:
I–V–vi–iii–IV–V–I
Arpeggiated Using
Mixed Rhythms

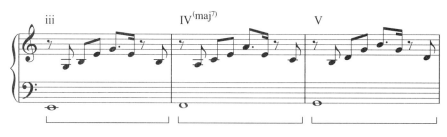

Hooks

Hooks are important in both pop and rock music. Sometimes rock is less hook-oriented, especially when it is focused on jamming. For example, most songs by The Grateful Dead are jam-oriented rather than hook-oriented.

Any song that hopes to get on Top 40 radio needs a hook of some sort. A hook's job is literally to "hook you in." Specifically, a hook is a repetitious melodic line that is almost always sung. The Beatles tune, "She Loves You" is a good example of a song with an infectious hook. Unlike most pop songs, this tune *begins* with the hook before moving into the first verse. Each chorus or refrain pounds the hook into your head until it's imprinted in your brain.

Try writing your own hooks. Here is a list of pop songs with strong hooks:

- "All You Need Is Love"—The Beatles
- "God Only Knows"—The Beach Boys
- "Piano Man"—Billy Joel
- "We Are the Champions"—Queen
- "Every Little Thing She Does Is Magic"—The Police
- "I Just Called to Say I Love You"—Stevie Wonder
- "Call Me"—Blondie
- "Thriller"—Michael Jackson
- "I'll Be There for You"—The Rembrandts (Theme from *Friends*)

How do you end a pop song? Sixth chords can be used to spice up any song ending, and they were used a lot in pop, country, and rock-n-roll during the 1950s and early 1960s. For example, "Blue Suede Shoes" by Carl Perkins ends on a major sixth chord and so does the Beatles tune "She Loves You." To play this chord, simply tack a major sixth on to a major triad. A C6 chord would include the notes C, E, G, and A. The "A" is the major sixth.

FIGURE 12-16:

I–vi–VI–V
Arpeggiated
with Left Hand
Crossover

Chapter 13
Rock-n-roll Piano Innovators

To understand rock piano, you will need to go back to its blues roots. Five pianists stand out in rock-n-roll's early history: Ray Charles, Fats Domino, Little Richard, Jerry Lee Lewis, and the lesser-known Johnnie Johnson. All five began as blues players. When reading about the pianists in this chapter, bear in mind the social climate in which this music was created. Analyzing artists from a historical perspective will help you to gain deeper access into the blues, R&B, jazz, country, and rock-n-roll.

The Dawning of a New Era

After World War II, a new style of music began to emerge in the American South that combined electric blues, gospel, and jump blues with folk and country and western. By the early 1950s, this music would be known distinctly as rock-n-roll.

Unlike the pop music of the 1930s and 1940s, rock was rowdy and obstreperous. It challenged the image of the matinee idol and the debonair crooner. Instead of offering audiences a clean-cut singer in a conservative suit, rock shocked audiences with suggestive dancing and greased-up pompadour hairstyles. By the mid-1950s, the James Dean movie *Rebel Without a Cause* came to symbolize angst and disobedience for a whole generation of kids.

FACT

The term *rhythm and blues* was invented by Jerry Wexler at Atlantic Records to replace the dubious phrase *race records*, which was used by industry folk to describe blues, gospel, and jazz recordings made by black artists. Modern R&B has little in common with R&B from the 40s and 50s.

At the same time, the United States was in the midst of the civil rights movement in which a different kind of disobedience (civil) was being carried out on buses and in restaurants, schools, and other public places. It's no wonder that rock would emerge on a parallel course. In truth, race has always complicated music in the United States. Rock's sudden marketability made these complexities especially transparent as white artists, producers, and promoters gained control of an art form that was primarily black. These days, rock is quite detached from its 1950s roots and its stars are overwhelmingly white, but it wasn't always this way. In the early days, the blues was rock's lynchpin and that meant heavy involvement from African-Americans.

Ray Charles

Born in 1930, Ray Charles is considered by many to be the father of rhythm and blues. Categorizing Charles can be difficult since he has great crossover appeal. He was influenced by the music of Charles Brown and Nat "King" Cole and by the pulsating boogie-woogie trio of Meade "Lux" Lewis, Albert Ammons, and Pete Johnson. Midway through his career, Charles's material also began to emulate white country artists, culminating in the album *Modern Sounds in Country and Western Music*, Volumes I and II (1962). This was followed up two decades later by a duet with outlaw country star Willie Nelson on "Seven Spanish Angels" (1984).

Charles was a consummate performer who experimented with musical styles. However, he was criticized for his forays into pop music and especially for endorsing Pepsi-Cola in TV advertisements. Charles never played "rock" per se, but his status as a pop icon places him in this chapter as well as in Chapter 11.

Ray Charles has had an enormous impact on rock and pop musicians, many of whom are legends in their own right. Singers such as Steve Winwood, Van Morrison, Joe Cocker, Stevie Wonder, Billy Joel, Rod Stewart, and the Rolling Stones have all cited Charles as an important influence.

Without a doubt, Charles's piano playing helped to define R&B as we know it. His early recordings often used horn riffs and funky grooves to complement his percussive chordal work. Examples of this include "What I'd Say, Parts I and II," "Sticks and Stones," "One Mint Julep," and others. During this era, a lick that Charles loved to play was a repetitive right-hand pattern similar to the one indicated in **FIGURE 13-1**.

This lick can be used between any minor third interval such as E and G, D and F, A and C, and so forth. Be careful of the fast-moving grace notes. Don't let them interrupt the flow of the rhythm in the main notes.

FIGURE 13-1:
Ray Charles Riff

Charles was a master blues player too, and his ability to capture the spirit of the blues in his pop and country repertoire was a special talent that sets him apart from many of his contemporaries. The twelve-bar blues in **FIGURE 13-2** mimics Brother Ray's approach to the blues. This is a slow blues, which can also be sped up and played using "straight eighths" if you prefer.

ALERT!

The musical examples in this chapter only approximate the playing styles of each artist. The goal with this chapter is to simply expose you to some legendary pianists and to give you a taste of each pianist's approach to music. You should further examine each of these five pianists through active listening and through other published resources (see Appendix B).

Since Hoagie Carmichael's "Georgia on My Mind" is so ingrained in the Ray Charles style, a spinoff has also been provided for your perusal. The harmonies in **FIGURE 13-3** are rather jazzy. You will see harmonic extensions, a suspension, and chord inversions. Some attempt has been made to simplify this musical example, but it's important to note that Charles was also fluent in jazz, so some fancy chords have been used here. Don't worry if you don't understand the nuts and bolts of the theory behind this chord progression. Just try playing this exercise, take note of the voicings, and see where your ear takes you when attempting to create similar passages.

FIGURE 13-2: Ray Charles–Style Blues

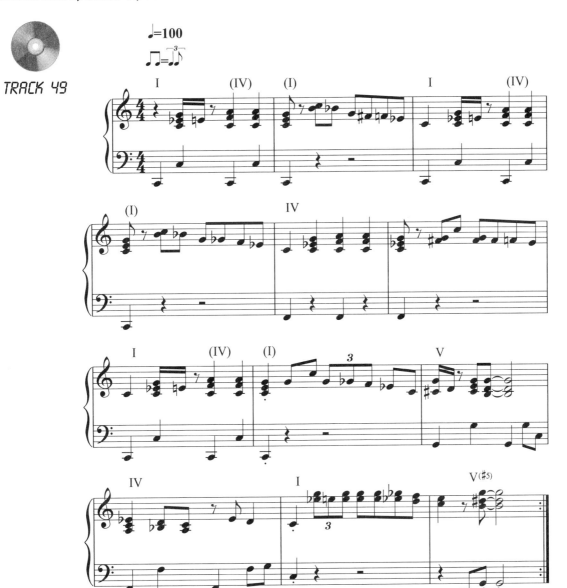

TRACK 49

FIGURE 13-3:

"Georgia on My Mind" Spinoff

TRACK 50

Fats Domino

Born in 1928, Antoine "Fats" Domino is one of the most important R&B and rock-n-roll icons on any instrument. A New Orleans native, Domino arrived on the scene with "The Fat Man" in 1949. Many considered this song to be the first rock-n-roll tune in history. Domino himself never cared much about the distinction between rock-n-roll and rhythm and blues. Instead, he simply focused on his unique sound, which combined elements of stride, boogie-woogie, and other blues styles.

Unlike Ray Charles, Domino's style never changed much. However, his consistency as a performer allowed him great staying power in a fickle industry. The pianist also possessed a friendly and smooth-toned voice, which helped him sell more albums than any other black artist in the pre-Beatles era. Another reason for this was his keen relationship with producer, trumpeter, and songwriter Dave Bartholomew. Together the Domino-Bartholomew team scored many Top 40 hits. Some of these songs include "Ain't That a Shame," "I'm Walking," "Blue Monday," and "Blueberry Hill."

Fats Domino and the Beatles had a long-running musical relationship. The inspiration for the Beatles' song "I Want to Hold Your Hand" is believed to be a line in Domino's "I Want to Walk You Home." In 1968, the Beatles modeled their song "Lady Madonna" on Fats Domino's style, along with Humphrey Lyttelton's 1956 hit "Bad Penny Blues." Domino returned the compliment in 1970 by covering "Lady Madonna."

Domino is probably best remembered for his triplet piano feel, which can also be thought of as a 12/8 ballad. The two terms are interchangeable. This style influenced a decade or more of rock-n-roll balladry. **FIGURE 13-4** shows you a basic rock chord progression using triplets.

FIGURE 13-4: Basic Rock Ballad

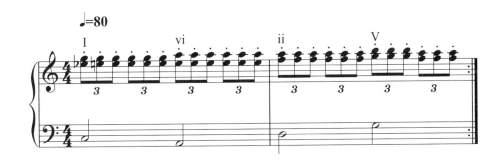

FIGURE **13-5** shows you a souped-up version of the same chord progression. The difference between the two progressions lies only in the left hand movement.

FIGURE **13-6** emulates Domino's 12/8 style. For this exercise, a full twelve-bar blues has been written. The bass line is typical of Domino, who used it on "Blueberry Hill" and other selections throughout his career. Typically, a horn section or guitarist would double the left hand.

It would be unfair to cite only Domino's 12/8 ballad style. He was a dynamic performer who also played up-tempo shuffles and other styles very effectively. FIGURE **13-7** illustrates the kind of driving shuffle feel that Domino might have used on any number of tunes. ("The Fat Man" is a good example of this.) The four-bar excerpt is a Domino shuffle. You'll notice that it's quite boogie-woogie influenced. Try working this pattern into a full twelve-bar blues.

FIGURE 13-5: Intermediate Rock Ballad

TRACK 51

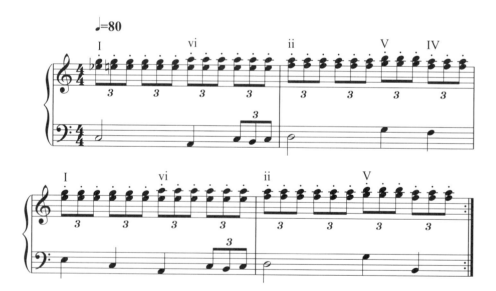

FIGURE 13-6: Fats Domino Slow Blues

TRACK 52

FIGURE 13-7: Fats Domino Shuffle

TRACK 53

Little Richard

Born in 1932, Richard Penniman was destined to become one of rock-n-roll's most important celebrities. A bubbly, flamboyant man, Little Richard was one of the most energetic rockers of his day. Unlike Fats Domino, Richard belted most of his lyrics, and he always sang with a coarse, raspy voice. Throughout his career, Richard was in conflict with himself, largely due to his Seventh Day Adventist upbringing. The pianist's wild, glitzy, and even outrageous image hardly complemented the life of a devout Christian. Consequently, his music underwent constant transformation. He would switch from rock-n-roll to gospel and then back again several times.

Richard's recordings for Specialty Records (1955–1957) are widely considered to be his most important. This text will not deal with Richard's gospel music, although it is well wrought and beautiful in its own right. As a rock pianist, you will want to concentrate more on Richard's two-year tenure at Specialty. There, he recorded such classics as "Tutti Frutti," "Long Tall Sally," "Jenny, Jenny," and "Good Golly, Miss Molly."

FIGURE 13-8:
Little Richard
Rock-n-Roll
Pattern

FIGURE 13-8 shows you an example of Little Richard's piano style, which is boogie-woogie based. Like players such as Meade "Lux" Lewis, Richard always played with a driving pulse. In other words, the eighth notes that appear in the exercise should really crackle. In order to do this, use big forearm chords.

Little Richard was also fond of playing rapid, machine gun–like triplets with his right hand. These can be difficult to play at first, so don't hesitate to slow the following exercises while practicing. Eventually, you will need to build up your stamina because these licks are intended to be played fast. Practicing with a metronome is a good idea when learning these triplet figures (see Chapter 17). **FIGURE 13-9** shows you one possible triplet pattern using the right hand only. **FIGURE 13-10** adds a basic boogie-woogie left hand. Rather than sixth intervals, as used in **FIGURE 13-9**, this exercise uses octaves with a stacked fifth in the right hand.

FIGURE 13-9:
Triplet Riff
Using Sixth
Intervals

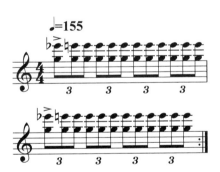

Like most '50s rock-n-rollers, Little Richard did perform some mellower material. These songs were known as "slow songs" or "slow dances" at sock-hops. Slow songs were not Richard's forte, but when he played them, he still knew how to enchant listeners. To hear Richard play a beautiful 12/8 ballad, check out "Send Me Some Lovin'" also culled from the Specialty Records era.

FIGURE 13-10: Octave Triplet Riff with Left Hand Added

TRACK 54

Jerry Lee Lewis

In Chapter 11, Memphis, Tennessee, was listed as one of America's blues capitals. It was also the home to Sam Phillips's legendary Sun Records. At Sun, musicians such as Elvis Presley, Roy Orbison, Johnny Cash, Carl Perkins, and others got their start. Jerry Lee Lewis was another young talent who hit the big time after recording for Sun.

Born in Louisiana in 1935, Lewis was exposed to both country and blues music as a youngster. Like Little Richard, Lewis was brought up a devout Christian. However, the young pianist cared more about boogie-woogie and "devil's music" than he did hymnals. This led to his expulsion from Bible school in Texas.

Lewis recorded his first single in 1954. However, it was Jack Clement who cemented Lewis's fame by signing him to Sun Records two years later. In 1957, Lewis became a teen idol scoring big with "Whole Lotta Shakin' Goin' On" and "Great Balls of Fire." However, scandal in England over his marriage to a cousin proved fatal to his reputation. This was soon followed by alcohol and drug addictions, health problems, and other personal tragedies. All of this sidetracked a very promising career. By the late 1960s, Lewis switched from rock-n-roll to country, hoping to find some renewed success. This decision paid off in 1972 when Lewis earned a number-one country hit with his version of "Chantilly Lace."

Nicknamed "The Killer," Lewis was one of rock's first bad boys. He toted guns, got into trouble with the law, and went wild on stage. He was known

FIGURE 13-11: Jerry Lee Lewis Boogie-Woogie

TRACK 55

for standing on pianos, sitting on the keys, dancing as he played, and other histrionics. Despite these gimmicks, Lewis was a skilled pianist, which is apparent on both his rock-n-roll and country albums.

FACT

Jerry Lee Lewis has two famous cousins. One is the former televangelist Jimmy Swaggart and the other is the country singer Mickey Gilley. In 1988, Reverend Swaggart's reputation took a nosedive due to an affair with a prostitute. Once again, Lewis's family was in the spotlight for scandalous reasons. During this time, Lewis was making a comeback on the rock-n-roll oldies circuit.

The following figure shows one boogie-woogie pattern that Lewis might have played during his rock years. If the left hand eighth notes are too fast, try simplifying them by playing quarter notes on beats one, two, and three. You will still need to play the eighth notes (A and G) on beat four.

You may have guessed that Lewis liked to play fast. This is true. Like Little Richard, speed and energy were integral to his sound. However, many of his songs are really just pumped-up blues numbers and the licks he plays draw largely from pianists like Albert Ammons and others. As you have seen in previous examples in this chapter, rock-n-roll piano uses a lot of roots, fifths, octaves, and sixths. Often these are played as rapid-fire sixteenth notes or triplets. There are other clichés, too. **FIGURE 13-12** shows you a repetitive

FIGURE 13-12:
Right-Hand Riff

right-hand pattern that Jerry Lee Lewis might have played. This would be played over a C or I chord (in the key of C major). This lick is fast, so again, learn it smoothly at a slower tempo before you try playing up-tempo. Clean, articulate playing is the objective here.

FIGURE 13-13:
Triplet Riff

Note: The 2,1 fingerings are played by the LEFT hand and the 1,3 fingerings are played by the RIGHT hand.

Another pattern that Jerry Lee Lewis might have played is shown in **FIG-URE 13-13**. This pattern uses both hands in the middle register of the piano. Be sure to note the fingerings and give this lick a percussive feel. In other words, don't play the notes too legato or pretty. Play them loud and staccato.

Jerry Lee Lewis was also very fond of glissandos. He often played big glissandos up and down the white and black keys of the keyboard. Lewis used his hands, elbows, feet, and even his buttocks (yes, his butt) to play glissandos, but unless you plan on being a showman in the Lewis style, it's recommended that you use only your hands! As discussed in Chapter 10, glissandos can be played many different ways. Obviously, the prim and proper classical glissando is not necessary here. The bottom and top notes indicated for the start and stop points of the glissando also do not need to be exact. Simply drag your hand up or down the keys as indicated, make sure you don't lose the beat, and play the other (nonglissando) notes accurately. In this style of music, the glissandos should be a little loose and carefree. Let 'em fly.

FIGURE 13-14: Glissandos

TRACK 56

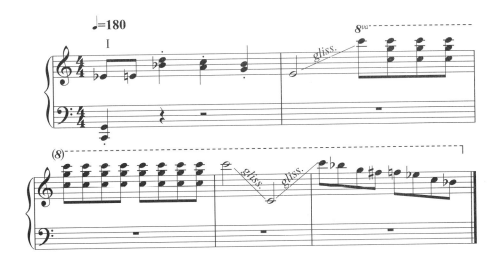

Last, a generic rock-n-roll comping pattern is included here. This is a simple roots/fifth phrase that is used by players like Little Richard, Jerry Lee Lewis, and others when they are essentially "marking time" at a fast speed. For example, Lewis would use this pattern when he was concentrating on his singing. **FIGURE 13-15** shows you how to do this over a C chord. Over an F chord, you would use the notes F (in octaves) and C. Over a G chord, you would use the notes G (in octaves) and D.

FIGURE 13-15:
Generic Rock-n-roll Comping

Can be transposed to IV or V chords too!

Johnnie Johnson

Johnnie Johnson is only recently getting his due. A relatively obscure pianist, Johnson's contributions to rock-n-roll should not be overlooked. Johnson was a West Virginia native who settled in St. Louis where he met and hired a young guitarist named Chuck Berry. Soon thereafter, Johnson's friendship with Berry would bloom into a long-lived musical collaboration.

As you probably know, Chuck Berry would go on to become one of rock-n-roll's most important icons, influencing everybody from the Beatles to the Rolling Stones, and Eric Clapton to Bruce Springsteen. Session pianist Lafayette Leake performed on some of Berry's Chess Records recordings, but it was Johnson who would become Berry's chief musical sidekick. In fact, the two men worked together—almost exclusively—for thirty years. During this time, a strong musical simpatico developed through hits such as "Roll Over Beethoven" and "No Particular Place to Go." Berry even wrote a tribute to Johnson called "Johnnie B. Goode."

QUESTION?

What makes Johnson's playing special?
Johnson's style is smooth and graceful. His hands seem to glide effortlessly over the keyboard. The blues lines he plays draw largely from the St. Louis and Chicago schools and he uses a lot of sixths and thirds in his solos. His style is also playful and rhythmically diverse.

Johnson's musical ideas influenced Berry from the very beginning, and the two men collaborated on more than fifty tunes. This eventually led to legal disputes between them, but this doesn't detract from the wonderful music they created together. Like all rock-n-roll pianists, Johnson's style was blues based. He really got a chance to shine on his 1992 solo release *Johnnie B. Bad*, which features the pianist performing with such notables as Keith Richards and Eric Clapton. On this release, Johnnie proves his greatness as a soloist. He also reaffirms his sterling accompaniment skills.

FIGURE 13-16 shows you an example of what Johnson might have played when jamming over a C major blues. A four-bar phrase is included with the first measure of the IV chord (measure five). You may want to learn this phrase and then complete the form with your own Johnson-influenced improvisation. When soloing, try to use repetition and call and response.

Repeating lines (musical phrases) helps the listener latch on to what you're playing. It also shows some thoughtfulness and confidence. When you repeat a lick, it's as if you're saying to the audience, "Hey, check this out. This is a good one!" Call and response, as described in Chapter 10, also helps create a meaningful dialogue between your phrases. This translates into surefooted soloing because you will build off one idea rather than a slew of random musical thoughts.

FIGURE 13-16: Playful Blues Licks

TRACK 57

Chapter 14

The Development of Rock

By the 1960s, rock-n-roll began to mature and grow into a well-defined style. Blues, R&B, and country music still influenced this new sound, but the end result was wholly rock. In fact, the full name rock-n-roll was eventually dropped as new artists sought to distance themselves from the first wave of rock-n-rollers. Nothing epitomized this better than the British Invasion, which was jump-started by the Beatles in 1964.

THE EVERYTHING ROCK & BLUES PIANO BOOK

THE EVERYTHING ROCK & BLUES PIANO BOOK

The Beatles

The Beatles are an anomaly in musical history. There have been many superstars in rock. However, no other rock star can match the popularity and enduring legacy of the Beatles. The Beatles raised the bar on popular music, generating a corpus of work that boasts dozens of classics. From "I Want to Hold Your Hand" to "A Hard Day's Night," "All You Need Is Love" to "The Long and Winding Road," the Beatles have captivated listeners with infectious melodies, indelible hooks, imaginative lyrics, brilliant arrangements, and creative musicianship. Given their manifold influence on popular music, it is in your best interest to get to know their discography and also the solo albums of John Lennon, Paul McCartney, and George Harrison.

Because of George Martin, Beatles arrangements often emulated European classical music. Martin's harpsichord solo on "In My Life" stands out as one of the group's finest instrumental interludes. This solo uses counterpoint between the right and left hands and its construction and development is inspired by the baroque fugue.

Producer and arranger George Martin is often viewed as the fifth Beatle. The main songwriters were Lennon and McCartney, although Harrison wrote many gems and drummer Ringo Starr wrote the song "Octopus's Garden." As stated in Chapter 1, the Beatles first emulated 1950s rock-n-roll styles. However, they quickly began developing their own voice. Each year, they reached new, creative heights, and their innovations stunned fans and critics alike.

Beatles songs always included tasty harmonic twists and thoughtful vocal harmonies, but this alone would not have made them legendary. One of their most enduring contributions is their use of the recording studio. During the psychedelic era (late 1960s), they began using the recording studio as an instrument. They rolled tape backward and varied the speed of tape machines. They used unorthodox microphone placements and experimented with sound processors to create unusual vocal and instrumental effects. They layered orchestral and non-Western instruments (such as the sitar and tabla drums) on top of guitars and were early users of electronic keyboards.

Paul McCartney and John Lennon both played the piano and composed frequently on this instrument. Some examples of Beatles piano styles are presented here. For further study, it is strongly recommended that you buy one of the many Beatles songbooks that exist. For example, Hal Leonard's *Beatlemania,* volumes I and II, are great resources (see Appendix B). If you want to understand pop and rock song construction, learn the repertoire of the Beatles. There is no better source.

In **FIGURE 14-1**, you will see the riff Paul McCartney uses on "Drive My Car" from the album *Yesterday…and Today* (1966). This is a stock blues riff, but it's used effectively between phrases on the song's chorus.

You can build this riff into a blues by simply transposing it to fit a IV chord and a V chord. **FIGURE 14-2** shows this riff used on an eight-bar modified blues. The rhythm has been changed slightly just to give it a funkier feel. It would be very simple to elongate this form to create a standard twelve-bar blues. Use other twelve-bar blues from this book (see Chapters 9 and 15) as your guide.

FIGURE 14-1:
"Drive My Car"
Riff

The Beatles loved using drop-down or step-down bass patterns. The following example is a simulation of something Paul McCartney might have played on a bridge. It is written in A minor, the relative minor of C major. This figure looks harmonically difficult, but it's really not all that fancy. Use your ear when playing drop-down patterns and experiment with different ideas of your own. In most cases, you will hear when a progression sounds harmonically correct.

FIGURE 14-2: Eight-Bar Blues

TRACK 58

FIGURE 14-3: Beatles Drop-down Bass Progression

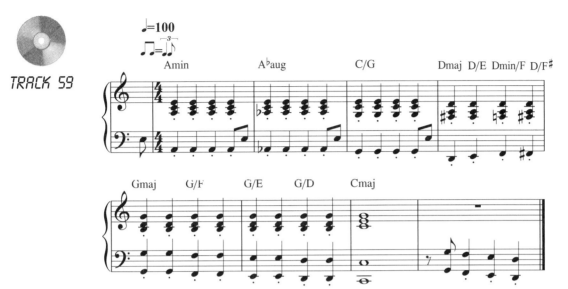

TRACK 59

The Doors

The Doors were a pivotal American rock band in the late 1960s and early 1970s. Despite the iconic stature of singer Jim Morrison, the Doors' style was largely centered on keyboardist Ray Manzarek, who filled the role of both accompanist and bass player. Using a Vox Continental organ and a Fender Rhodes Piano Bass, he played chords and melodies with his right hand and bass lines with his left.

A cofounder of the band, Manzarek defined the Doors' sound on songs such as "Break on Through," "Light My Fire," "Hello, I Love You," and many more. Along with guitarist Robbie Krieger and drummer John Densmore, Manzarek brought balance and counterpoint to Morrison's often unstable fiery performances. More than any other member, Manzarek was the glue that held the Doors' music together.

Manzarek redefined the role of the keyboardist in popular music. His playing showed great dexterity, steadiness, and independence, and he always kept rock-solid bass lines going even when he was soloing overtop.

Manzarek's solos were usually modal soliloquies that borrowed from jazz, most notably the work of John Coltrane, Thelonious Monk, and Herbie Hancock. Yet, his playing never comes across overtly as jazz because Manzarek rarely used the language of bebop. Instead, he focused on post-bop modal and diatonic explorations.

FIGURE 14-4 emulates Manzarek's style, especially as he played on "Light My Fire" from the self-titled album *The Doors* (1967). The notes used in the right hand outline an A Dorian scale: A, B, C, D, E, F#, G, A. If you wish to get fancy, you may use a B Dorian scale on the B minor chord, which would include the notes C# and G#. You may also play with A and B minor pentatonics, respectively. If you've forgotten any of these scales, see Chapter 5.

FIGURE 14-4: Ray Manzarek Modal Solo

TRACK 60

Progressive Rock

British progressive rock (or prog-rock) was popular throughout the 1970s, appealing primarily to "arena rock" and "stoner" audiences. Prog-rock is very listener oriented—as opposed to being oriented toward dancers—and it often features lengthy, multipart compositions. Prog-rock borrows from diverse musical genres including jazz, folk, electric blues, heavy metal, and avant-garde. More often than not, it also draws from European classical, and many of its practitioners are well-trained virtuosos.

Prog-rock was influenced early on by the Beatles' psychedelic experiments, especially the pioneering album *Sgt. Pepper's Lonely Hearts Club Band*. However, prog-rock would ultimately embrace structural and metric complexity over pop hooks, causing some listeners to deem it excessive and self-important.

The first prog-rock album was arguably *In the Court of the Crimson King* by King Crimson (1969). This album featured keyboards and mellotron by Ian Mac-Donald. Over the next decade, keyboards would continue to define prog-rock. Four keyboardists would eventually dominate this scene: Rick Wakeman (Yes), Keith Emerson (Emerson, Lake and Palmer), Tony Banks (Genesis), and Richard Wright (Pink Floyd). Prog-rock continues to thrive today with select audiences.

More than any others, keyboardists Keith Emerson and Rick Wakeman have become synonymous with prog-rock. Both are classically trained and both are known for having vast arrays of keyboards, organs, and synthesizers in their stage setups. They were also unique showmen who often used stage antics to heighten their already flashy technical displays.

FIGURE 14-5 shows you an example of something Keith Emerson might have played. It draws from both "contemporary classical" and modern jazz, and it employs a number of harmonic twists, including a spicy E7#9 at the end that you should remember from Chapter 7.

FIGURE 14-5: Keith Emerson Harmonic Adventurousness

TRACK 61

FIGURE 14-6: Rick Wakeman Solo

FIGURE 14-6 is an example of something Rick Wakeman might have played. It is a dramatic, minor keyed example that revolves around power chords and a natural minor scale. Power chords contain only roots and fifths. These chords retain the diatonic function of a chord, but by omitting the third scale degree, they leave the major or minor quality of a chord ambiguous. The "power" comes from the harmonic consonance of a perfect fifth interval.

FACT

The mellotron is a polyphonic keyboard sampler developed in England during the early 1960s. The mellotron's sound bank comprises prerecorded instruments (captured on magnetic tape strips). Strings, brass, flutes, and other orchestral instruments were commonly sampled for use. Each tape contains around eight seconds of playing time. The mellotron is an important forerunner to the digital sampler.

Stevie Wonder

If Ray Charles is the father of R&B, Stevie Wonder might be considered the first son. Along with Marvin Gaye, Wonder stands out as one of the most important black performers of his generation. He is also one of the most celebrated pop stars since the rock-n-roll age. As of this writing, Wonder's career boasts nine number-one hits, and he has sold more than 100 million records.

Born in Saginaw, Michigan, in 1950, Wonder was a precocious child with an incredible ear for music. Before high school, he was signed to Motown Records where he scored his first number-one hit "Fingertips" in 1963. At age twenty, Wonder began pouring out the singles. Some of these included "For Once in My Life," "My Cherie Amour," and "Signed, Sealed, Delivered (I'm Yours)." Later albums *Innervisions*, *Songs in the Key of Life*, and the soundtrack to *The Woman in Red* also yielded major hits, establishing Wonder as a musical tour de force.

Like Ray Charles, Wonder borrowed from a variety of genres. He studied classical piano but was influenced more by black art forms. Blues, Motown, R&B, soul, funk, reggae, and jazz were all incorporated into his sound. A multi-instrumentalist, Wonder often played drums, hand percussion, and bass; he also distinguished himself on the harmonica. Despite his skill on a number of instruments, Wonder's main focus was always on playing piano (or keyboards) and songwriting.

"Superstition," is a song that shot to number one in 1972. On this tune, Wonder uses a clavinet. A clavinet is an electronic keyboard that mimics the sound of a harpsichord. **FIGURE 14-7** shows you a simplified version of a funk groove Wonder might have played on "Superstition." Be careful of the rhythms, particularly the syncopated "e" of two. It's best to play this exercise slowly at first while counting out loud. This figure is written in the key of C minor (three flats).

Wonder also wrote jazzy tunes that used sophisticated harmonies and gorgeous hooks. His 1973 number-one hit, "You Are the Sunshine of My Life," is a perfect example of this. **FIGURE 14-8** is a spinoff on this tune's chord progression. The chords used here are not identical to the ones used in the song, but they show the kind of lush harmonization Wonder was capable of producing. Don't forget to use the pedal as indicated.

FIGURE 14-7: Stevie Wonder Clavinet

TRACK 62

FIGURE 14-8: Stevie Wonder Jazzy Chords

TRACK 63

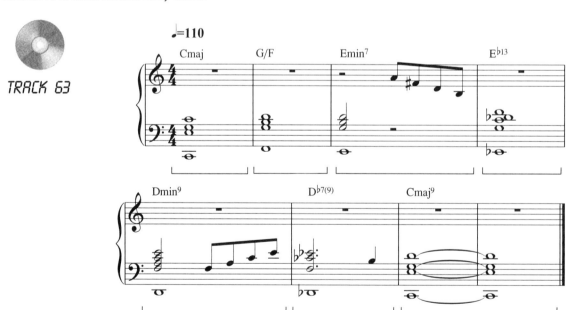

Southern Rock

Although Jerry Lee Lewis, Elvis Presley, Little Richard, and other 1950s rock-n-rollers came from the American South, they do not fit in the Southern rock category. It wasn't until after the British Invasion that Southern rock would be officially born. Influenced by roots rockers Credence Clearwater Revival and the Band, Southern rock peaked in the 1970s with the success of the Allman Brothers Band, Lynyrd Skynyrd, ZZ Top, the Charlie Daniel's Band, Alabama, and others. Southern rock should not be confused with its close cousin, heartland rock, which is best typified by the music of John Mellencamp.

ALERT!

Generally, Southern rock mixes folk, country and western, and blues with driving rhythms and crunchy guitars. Lyrically, Southern rock often embraces the values and symbols of the American Confederacy or Rebel South. It also tends to promote "good ole boy" and redneck stereotypes.

In its prime, keyboards, organ, and piano were all commonplace in Southern rock. Arguably, the two most important keyboardists in this sub-genre were Billy Powell (Lynyrd Skynyrd) and Gregg Allman (The Allman Brothers Band). Also, in the 1980s ZZ Top showed how Southern rock could be combined with synth-pop. This is apparent on the albums *Eliminator* (1981) and *Afterburner* (1985), both of which prominently feature synthesizers and sequencers.

Lynyrd Skynyrd and the Allman Brothers Band embraced the blues in their music. This is evident in the down-home organ playing of Allman and in the swampy piano riffs of Powell. Both players used blues clichés like the ones demonstrated in this book. So if you wish to play as they did, review Chapters 9, 10, and 11 to begin this process.

FIGURE 14-9 is an amalgamation of two of Billy Powell's riffs from the Southern rock anthem "Sweet Home Alabama." This lick, like many blues licks, uses an abundance of sixth intervals (see Chapter 11). Be careful of the fingerings in this figure. The left and right hands are quite integrated; suggested fingerings are indicated.

FIGURE 14-9:

Billy Powell Riff

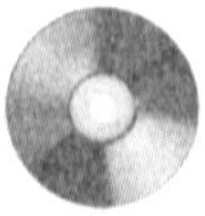

TRACK 64

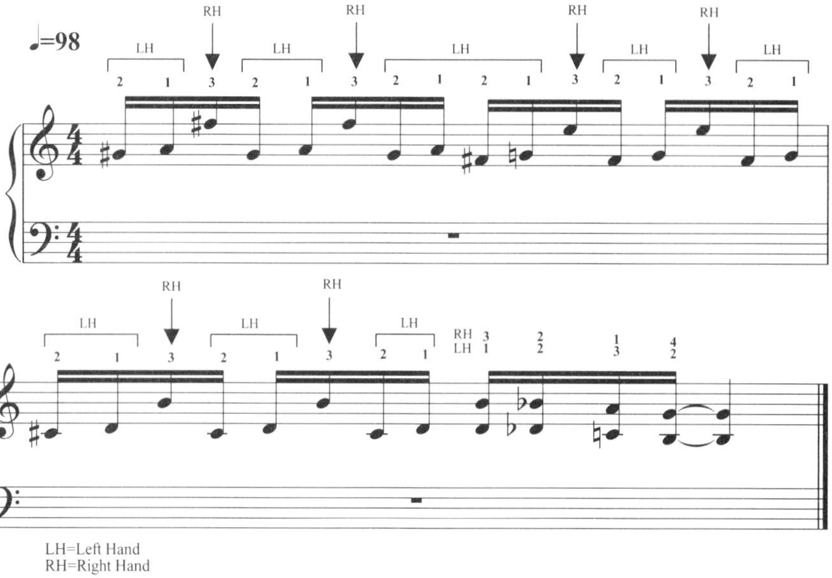

LH=Left Hand
RH=Right Hand

Synth-Pop

Synthesizers have been used in pop and rock music since the 1960s. However, they did not become the focus until the early 1980s, when keyboards became portable and musicians became more aware of the digital age.

At this time, a second British invasion was taking place, and a sleek keyboard-based style of pop hit the Top 40. This was epitomized by such acts as Duran Duran, Gary Numan, the Cure, Eurythmics, Depeche Mode, Erasure, Flock of Seagulls, Spandau Ballet, and Culture Club. Early on, synth-pop borrowed largely from electronic art music. The music of Kraftwerk was particularly influential. This German ensemble almost single-handedly revolutionized sequenced music. Kraftwerk began experimenting with electronic soundscapes as early as 1970. By the early 2000s, they were still leading the way, employing laptops and other technology. Brian Eno was another important figure in synth-pop. His creative use of synthesizers and other electronic media made Roxy Music one of the most important art rock groups in the early 1970s. Eno's attention to nuance, texture, color, and mood also ushered in a new style of electronic music called Ambient.

Broadly, synth-pop could fit under the umbrella of New Wave, which is a term that describes the third significant movement in rock. (The first "wave" was characterized by 1950s rock-n-roll; the second "wave" was characterized by the British Invasion of the 1960s.) New Wave includes music from the second British invasion. It also includes select American artists. Among them are Talking Heads, R.E.M., Devo, and Tom Petty. The latter even claimed to have created the genre with his album *You're Gonna Get It!* (1978).

Ambient music uses synthesizers and other devices to create a musical atmosphere. Eno's music can exist in the foreground or the background; it can be both captivating and ignorable. Ambient music culls largely from minimalism and the music of French composer Erik Satie.

FIGURE 14-10 is an example of how keyboards might have been used in synth-pop. Often, synth parts were layered in the studio, so this practice is emulated in this exercise. **FIGURE 14-10** shows four layered synth voices, although more might have been used in real life. Notice how arpeggios are used. Some keyboards from the synth-pop era, like the Juno 60, could play arpeggios automatically—all you did was turn on the arpeggiator function and press a key. Harmonically, **FIGURE 14-10** uses a suspended second (C and D), which resolves to a major third (C and E). Play each line separately or in pairs.

Singer-Songwriters and Piano Pop

The term *singer-songwriter* refers to someone who writes their own songs and accompanies themselves on a guitar or piano. Originally, the term was applied only to folk and country artists. However, this label has now been stretched to embrace singers and songwriters of all types. The two most celebrated piano-based singer-songwriters are Elton John and Billy Joel. Randy Newman, Jackson Browne, and Joe Jackson are also vital piano-based singer-songwriters. Additionally, newer artists Tori Amos, Sarah McLaughlin, Rufus Wainwright, Fiona Apple, Vanessa Carlton, and Ben Folds continue to keep the singer-songwriter tradition alive.

These artists could also be considered "piano pop," a style where the piano is the central instrument as opposed to the classic four-piece rock lineup consisting of lead guitar, rhythm guitar, bass, and drums.

FIGURE 14-10: Synth-Pop Example

TRACK 65

Elton John

Born in 1947, Elton John remains one of the world's leading pop stars. As of this writing, the British singer has sold around 250 million albums. He also has fifty Top 40 hits. Although he is known as a pop stylist, John was influenced early on by gospel, boogie-woogie, and 1950s rock-n-roll. The latter is evident on the hit "Crocodile Rock." Like most of his contemporaries, John was also influenced by the Beatles. For example, "Goodbye Yellow Brick Road" draws inspiration from the Beatles' *Abbey Road*. Together with lyricist Bernie Taupin, John has written such megahits as "Bennie and the Jets," "Daniel," "Rocket Man," "Candle in the Wind," and many more.

Like other songwriters, John often uses the third scale degree in the bass. In most cases, the third scale degree acts as a leading tone to the root of the next chord. **FIGURE 14-11** (from "Goodbye Yellow Brick Road") illustrates this kind of harmonic movement. The lyric that is sung over this passage is "Going back to my plough." The song is in F major (one flat).

FIGURE 14-11:
Elton John
Harmonic
Movement

In this song, John also moves from a vi to a major III, then to a IV, and finally to a flat VI (borrowed chord). The flatted VI chord is a very effective harmonic twist (see Chapter 6). This is shown in **FIGURE 14-12**.

FIGURE 14-12:
Flattened VI
ChordProgression

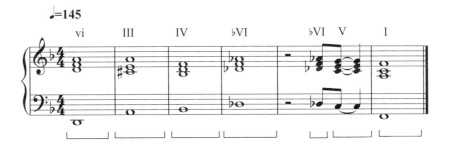

Billy Joel

Born in 1949, Billy Joel is perhaps the only piano-pop artist who can rival Elton John. Raised in Long Island, Joel hit it big with the 1973 album

Piano Man, which became his first gold record. Often misunderstood as a sentimental pop stylist, Joel's songs often address anger, loneliness, and defiance. Moreover, his paeans to women, such as "She's Always a Woman" and "She's Got a Way," do more than romanticize the opposite sex. Rather, they illuminate the mysteries of love through simple poetic confessions. Influenced by a whole host of musical styles—from blues to European classical—Joel's discography boasts both sophistication and variety.

Joel is a musical chameleon. He is known for his doo-wop-inspired songs, Tin Pan Alley emulations, Beatles-influenced rock, and R&B salutes. **FIGURE 14-12** is an example of Billy Joel's R&B–influenced piano style. It is a spinoff on "New York State of Mind," which is Joel's homage to Ray Charles.

FIGURE 14-13: Billy Joel Harmonic Movement

Chapter 15
Study Pieces

In this chapter, you will play longer, more expansive pieces. The first half of the chapter focuses on blues study pieces, while the second half focuses on rock and pop. First, review the material in the first fourteen chapters before attempting these pieces. After you've worked your way through these pieces, try writing your own etudes. You may also use these compositions as a springboard for improvisation or songwriting.

What Is an Etude?

Etude means "study" in French and comes from the old French term *estudie*. In music, etudes are training or instructional pieces used to teach a particular technique or style. The etudes in this chapter utilize the techniques, styles, and theoretical elements discussed in earlier chapters. Overall, they are practical exercises designed to test your skill and knowledge.

Despite the pedagogical nature of these etudes, it is hoped that you will find these pieces enjoyable to listen to. Try performing them in front of an audience. Performing is critical to your musical development. No audience? Why not play these pieces for your friends and family? All you need is a piano or keyboard and a living room.

In general, these etudes represent the culmination of the ideas, techniques, and concepts learned in Chapters 1–14. It's time to bring it all together into one big package. In other words, it's time to coalesce your knowledge.

Analyzing Chords

None of the etudes in this chapter include chord symbols or roman numerals. This is purposeful. It's time for *you* to analyze chords on your own. The blues etudes will be pretty clear; they all use twelve-bar forms. The pop etude "For Kicks" may utilize a few chords that you haven't seen since the beginning of the book (see Chapter 6). However, with a little review, you should be able to figure out the harmonic underpinning of this piece. If you're still unsure, a generalized harmonic analysis of "For Kicks" is presented later in the chapter.

To figure out the chords to any piece of music, consider the bottom note or lowest pitch to be the root. Be careful of slash chords. For example, if you see that a clearly defined triad containing the notes C, E, G, and E is in the root you should recognize that this is a C triad with an E in the bass; this is written as C/E. Also, be aware that chords can be spelled in a variety of ways. It all depends on the context. As a result, chords are like homonyms. In language, homonyms are two or more words that have the same spelling but different meanings.

ALERT!

Don't get confused by passing tones, scalar runs, or atonal passages. What is atonal music? Atonal music has no key center. It often sounds random and mysterious. To avoid opening up a big can of worms, only tonal music has been used in this book. However, atonal music has been used quite effectively in art rock.

Once you've established the root, look for a third. The third tells you whether a chord is major or minor. If you analyze a chord and realize that it is not major or minor, it's probably augmented, diminished, or half-diminished. Review Chapter 6 for a better understanding of these types of chords. Another exception is power chords. These types of chords omit thirds altogether. Fifths are sometimes omitted from chords, too, because they are so consonant. Shell chords might also leave out thirds and fifths. For example, a shell chord might contain only a tonic and a minor seventh (e.g., C- and B-flat).

To name the other notes that appear in a chord, simply count scale degrees (see Chapter 4). Be mindful of diatonic notes versus altered tones. For example, flatted thirteenths and sharp nines are altered tones. Major sixths, sevenths, and ninths are diatonic notes. Also, familiarize yourself with the standard language used to describe altered tones. For example, musicians would never say "flat ten." They would always word this particular altered tone as "sharp nine."

Blues Etude #1: "Blues for Dr. John"

Blues Etude #1: "Blues for Dr. John" is an intermediate-to-difficult-level boogie-woogie. If you're still a relative beginner, you may want to skip this piece for now and come back to it when you've developed more technique and hand independence. If you think you've got what it takes, read on!

Dr. John (AKA Mac Rebennack) is one of the most famous blues pianists to emerge from New Orleans. As you read in Chapter 11, the Crescent City is a hotbed for piano blues. Dr. John is heavily influenced by such players as Champion Jack Dupree and Professor Longhair and is himself a part of this lineage of master bluesmen. His style combines R&B, early rock-n-roll, funk, and swamp grooves together with boogie-woogie and jazz. His jazz influences center on Duke Ellington and Thelonious Monk.

QUESTION?

Is Dr. Teeth from the Muppets band, Dr. Teeth and the Electric Mayhem, based on someone?
Apparently, Muppets founder Jim Henson was a big fan of the sharply dressed New Orleans pianist Dr. John. The Muppet Dr. Teeth even mimics Dr. John's raspy voice and uses musician's lingo when he talks.

Dr. John's piano style is smooth, flowing, and syncopated. He sometimes uses the following rhythmical motif: . You were introduced to this rhythm in **FIGURE 13-13**. Practice this pattern separately at first before incorporating it into the etude. In other words, practice this rhythm until it rolls off your fingertips with ease. It should not sound forced or staccato; rather, it should be attached and legato.

FIGURE 15-1: "Blues for Dr. John" Bass Line Without Octaves

FIGURE 15-2: Blues Etude #1: "Blues for Dr. John"

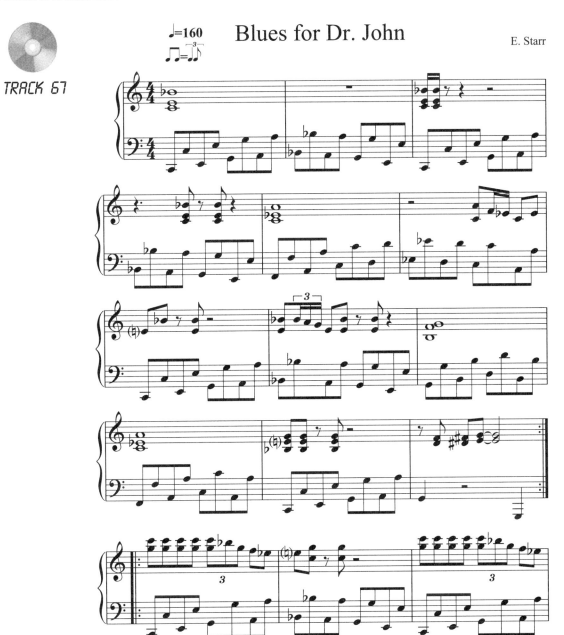

TRACK 67

♩=160

Blues for Dr. John

E. Starr

FIGURE 15-2 (continued): Blues Etude #1: "Blues for Dr. John"

FIGURE 15-2 (continued): Blues Etude #1: "Blues for Dr. John"

⌢ = Hold chord out (fermata symbol)

As previously mentioned, this etude is one of the more difficult pieces in this book. A big reason for this is the fancy left-hand pattern. As you will see, the left hand moves up and down the keyboard in octaves. As a result, you must play very accurately. There's nothing worse than a sloppy left hand when playing a boogie-woogie bass pattern. If you're having a difficult time playing the bass line in octaves, try simplifying it. The best way to do it is to take out the octaves altogether. Use the pattern in **FIGURE 15-1** (see page 220).

It is highly recommended that you learn the piece one hand at a time. When you're ready to put your hands together, play the etude at a slow tempo. Remember, clean, articulate playing is essential in boogie-woogie.

Blues Etude #2: "Tinsel Town Boogie"

Blues Etude #2: "Tinsel Town Boogie" uses the famous boogie-woogie bass line that was used in "Boogie Woogie Bugle Boy." This World War II anthem was first heard in the Abbot and Costello movie *Buck Privates* (1941). Since

FIGURE 15-3: Blues Etude #2: "Tinsel Town Boogie"

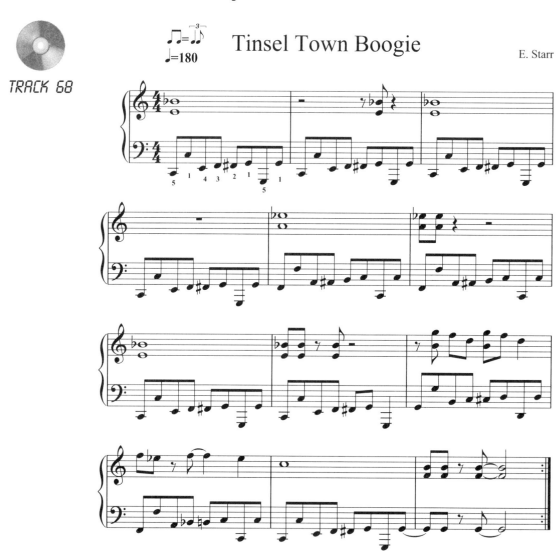

FIGURE 15-3 (continued): Blues Etude #2: "Tinsel Town Boogie"

FIGURE 15-3 (continued): Blues Etude #2: "Tinsel Town Boogie"

then, the song's bass line has become synonymous with boogie-woogie. In the tune's lyric, there is mention of "eight to the bar." *Eight to a bar* was a common phrase used in the 1940s to describe the driving eighth note rhythms played in the bass or left hand in boogie-woogie music.

True to form, the bass line in this etude uses eighth notes or "eight to the bar." Like "Blues for Dr. John," this piece requires significant independence between your hands. Once again, it is recommended that you practice slowly one hand at a time. Also, be careful of and consistent with the fingering in the left hand. The fingering in the left hand is the same on the I, IV, and V chords; it is written for you in the first measure. The right hand emulates horn riffs, which was a common way to conceive of soloing during the boogie era.

As you will notice, this etude is really a written improvisation. The right hand uses the blues scale throughout, and the ending employs a fancy C13 chord, which gives the tune extra tension and climax. Practice this piece with a metronome to ensure steady time (see Chapter 17). Most of all, remember that it is more important to play correctly and accurately than it is to play blazingly fast.

Blues Etude #3: "Lazy Blues"

Blues Etude #3: "Lazy Blues" is a slow blues with a walking bass line. Slow blues tunes can be hard to notate. This is because blues musicians usually use free rhythms. In other words, they will play with a superimposed rubato feel. Given this, melodic lines tend to float arrhythmically over the bar lines. In slow blues numbers, the tempo and time signature never waver, but the rhythms do not always divide and subdivide neatly. Instead, the rhythms accelerando and ritardando within the context of the groove. **FIGURE 15-4** (see page 228) shows one example of this. To understand this figure, you will need to listen to the CD to hear the gradual speeding up and slowing down of the sixteenth notes.

It's crucial that you know about free rhythms and their use in blues. To do this, you will have to listen carefully to this music (see Appendix A). Virtually all blues instrumentalists use free rhythms. However, since they are confusing on paper, they have been omitted in "Lazy Blues." For ease

FIGURE 15-4: Free Rhythms

TRACK 69

in reading and interpretation, all of the rhythms in this piece fit neatly into triple patterns. Still, it's important to perform this etude with a relaxed feel. Don't play these rhythms stiff. Unlike boogie-woogie, slow blues should not sound urgent or rushed. It should sound passionate yet logy, animated yet carefree.

Be careful of the triplet rolls. In this case, you will play four thirty-second note triplets per eighth note triplet. It's not as difficult as it sounds, but you may want to use a metronome to ensure accuracy. Start by playing stripped-down eighth note triplets. Once you feel confident with this rhythm, simply roll your fingers on the given pitches. You'll find that the pattern should fall under your fingertips quite easily. Make sure you don't lose the pulse of the eighth note triplets when rolling your fingers.

Rock Etude: "Solar Wind for Polyphonic Synthesizer"

"Solar Wind" (See **FIGURE 15-6** on page 233) is written for a synthesizer, but it can be played on the piano, too. If you do play it on a synth, you will need to use a modern polyphonic keyboard. As you will read in Chapter 16, early synthesizers are monophonic. This means that they play only one note at a time (no chords).

"Solar Wind" is intended to build technique. It is influenced by the progressive-rock era of the 1970s, specifically the music of Rick Wakeman (see Chapter 14). Since Wakeman and others like him borrowed from European classical, this piece emulates the two-hand counterpoint used in baroque music. However, this piece does not conform to the strict rules of fugal writing, so don't confuse it with authentic baroque music. This rock etude simply mimics the elements of the baroque style, specifically the fugues of J. S. Bach.

FIGURE 15-5: Blues Etude #3: "Lazy Blues"

TRACK 70

Lazy Blues

E. Starr

FIGURE 15-5 (continued): Blues Etude #3: "Lazy Blues"

FIGURE 15-5 (continued): Blues Etude #3: "Lazy Blues"

It is highly recommended that you study baroque repertoire in order to develop facile technique and an ear for musical counterpoint. The late Canadian pianist Glenn Gould is arguably the finest modern interpreter of J. S. Bach. It would be in your best interest to familiarize yourself with Gould's recordings. If you study players like Gould, you will learn a great deal about phrasing and interpreting music.

To play "Solar Wind," you will need to be proficient with minor scales and arpeggios (see Chapter 8). This piece is written in A minor. However, it does not use a natural G. Instead, it employs a G-sharp borrowing from the harmonic minor scale. The etude is based around an eight-bar harmonic progression, which bookends the piece. Take a moment to analyze the first eight measures and then pencil in the chords above the staff.

FACT

Baroque music flourished in Europe from roughly 1600 to 1760. The Renaissance period preceded it and the classical period followed. During the baroque era, Western harmony and tonality was standardized.

"Solar Wind" is a flashy etude that evokes the grandeur of the progressive-rock epic. However, as you will notice, this piece is a lot shorter than the average prog-rock classic. To lengthen it, try writing your own scalar/arpeggiated variations over the chords. You may also compose a melody that fits over the harmonic progression. After that, build a solo around your melodic elements. In classical, this would be called theme and variation. If you're really ambitious, try writing a bridge to this piece. Perhaps you could write a bridge that modulates into a major key.

Pop Etude: "For Kicks"

This chapter on rock and blues etudes would be incomplete without a piano pop etude. "For Kicks" (**FIGURE 15-7** on page 237) is a contemplative piano ballad that brings together many of the harmonic concepts discussed earlier in the book. The piece is in C major, but it modulates to its parallel minor at the end of measure nineteen. On measure twenty-nine, it switches back to C major with the reintroduction of the main theme. This theme is simply a two-measure hook or motif. It first appears in measures one and two, and it contains a flatted VI chord. On measure six, a deceptive cadence is used as the flatted VI chord resolves to an A minor (rather than a C major).

Other significant features include the use of major seventh chords on measure nine and measure forty-four. Further, the song uses a flatted VII

FIGURE 15-6: Rock Etude: "Solar Wind for Polyphonic Synthesizer"

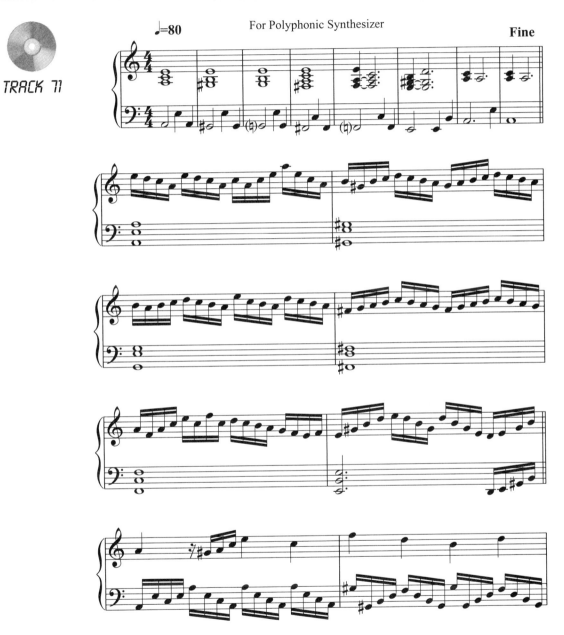

TRACK 71

FIGURE 15-6 (continued): Rock Etude: "Solar Wind for Polyphonic Synthesizer"

FIGURE 15-6 (continued): Rock Etude: "Solar Wind for Polyphonic Synthesizer"

chord (B-flat major) in several spots; it first appears in measure fifteen. Suspensions are also used throughout. For example, the main theme contains a D set against an A-flat major chord. This D is a suspended fourth. Like most suspended chords, it resolves down to the major third scale degree. The last two measures of the piece also employ suspensions. In this case, suspended twos are used. Like their suspended fourth cousins, the suspended twos in this etude resolve to a major third. Last, you will notice that a minor pentatonic is used in measures twenty and twenty-two, and a major pentatonic is used in measures thirty and thirty-three. (You should recall learning about pentatonics from Chapter 5.) Measure numbers are included at the beginning of each system for ease in referencing this text.

To hear expressive pop ballad piano playing, listen to pianists such as Joe Jackson, Billy Joel, and Elton John. Also, new age pianists are known for their soft-toned, warm ballad styles. Often criticized for being too saccharine or sentimental, new age pianists have nonetheless helped to keep the piano pop tradition alive.

"For Kicks" is intended to be a subtle, atmospheric piece. Therefore, when playing this etude, think about texture, color, and nuance. Feel free to use lots of dynamic swells and make sure your phrases always flow gently into one another. In order to make this piece really sing, you will need to use the sustain pedal, but be sure to follow the pedaling carefully. Sloppy pedaling will result in muddy and discordant phrases.

FIGURE 15-7: Pop Etude: "For Kicks"

For Kicks

E. Starr

TRACK 72

(see below for pedaling instructions)

Since this piece uses a lot of sustain, lines with "up" arrows have been used in place of brackets to help you pedal more accurately. The line (——) means to depress the pedal; the arrow (∧) shows the release points.

FIGURE 15-7 (continued): Pop Etude: "For Kicks"

FIGURE 15-7 (continued): Pop Etude: "For Kicks"

Chapter 16

Equipment to Meet Your Needs

Any good musician will tell you that equipment greatly affects your performance ability. For example, if you use an out-of-tune piano, you will not be able to play at your best. On the other hand, a $150,000 Bosendorfer will not make even the most dedicated beginners sound like pros. The same is true of keyboardists. Using the appropriate digital piano or synthesizer is essential to success. Buying the right equipment is really about balancing your needs and interests with a little common sense and a good dose of gear know-how.

The Piano

These days, most beginners purchase a keyboard rather than a piano. Because of the cost and the size, pianos are often impractical. However, some students still enjoy learning on pianos, and this should not be discouraged by teachers. Not even the finest keyboards can truly simulate a piano. The touch, response, and sound of a piano can never really be duplicated, because a piano is an acoustic instrument. A keyboard, on the other hand, is made out of plastic, and its sound is produced electronically.

A piano is composed of wood, metal, and felt. On good pianos, plastic is only used on the keys. The piano makes a sound when a key is pressed and an internal hammer strikes a set of three strings. (In the lower register, each hammer is assigned to only one string.) Because the strings are hit, the piano is considered a percussion instrument. The piano's hammers act like mallets or sticks, making it a cousin to the drum or to other mallet instruments such as the xylophone and marimba.

FACT

Before World War II, white keys were covered with bands of ivory hence the phrase *tickling the ole ivories*. Since ivory comes from the incisor teeth of endangered species, piano manufacturers have now switched to plastic strips. The difference in feel and texture is negligible.

The piano is designed to let its metal strings vibrate. The sustain pedal (see Chapter 4) lets them resonate fully. Moreover, the piano's construction allows for the creation of deep, rich tones, colors, and textures. Because of this, the piano is the most expressive keyboard instrument available. The piano's uniquely crowned sounding board gives it brilliant timbres (tone colors), which ultimately sets it apart from its electronic brethren. With the exception of some newfangled hybrids, electronic keyboards do not have a sounding board. Therefore, they can never fully reproduce the exquisite, full-bodied tone of a piano.

The piano is made up of many parts, both large and small. Some of the parts not previously mentioned include the iron frame, the damper, the action, the bridges, the key bed, and the lyre. These components are critical to the construction and design of the piano, but you needn't be an expert on all these parts. As long as you understand the basic mechanics of the piano, you will possess all the knowledge you need to get started. Just remember that the felt-tipped hammers strike the strings and the sounding board adds color and refinement to each note. The rest is in the hands of the pianist.

Keyboards and Synthesizers

Keyboards and synthesizers are useful items for pianists of all ages and stages. While they will never replace the piano, they can simulate a piano's sound and feel. Today, most keyboard companies manufacture eighty-eight-key keyboards. This is the size of a standard piano keyboard. The piano's case (large exterior shell) is discarded in keyboard design, but otherwise, the area viewed and used by the keyboardist is nearly the same. In other words, the keys are arranged on a keyboard exactly as they are on a piano. On professional keyboards, the actual key size and weight also remain the same. No matter what the model, the colors of the keys—black and white—are never altered.

Keyboards come in different shapes and sizes. Some companies even make roll-up keyboards. If you're a beginner, you'll want to make sure that your keyboard is fitted with full-size keys. Weighted or semi-weighted keys are also highly recommended.

Since digital keyboards deliver nearly the same feel and sound as a piano, students and pros alike have long enjoyed using them. What's more, modern keyboards offer a cache of electronic sounds, which add variety to any musical setting. These days, virtually every sound heard in music has a keyboard equivalent. For example, most keyboards can simulate the human voice, harpsichords, organs, string orchestras, guitars, flutes, clarinets, harps, banjos, French horns, glockenspiels, and much, much more. Other common sounds include bongo and conga drums, timpani, clapping, ocean waves, gunshots, car horns, birds chirping, glass breaking, and other harebrained sound effects. Many companies even offer whole sound libraries, which contain hundreds of presets.

How good are the sounds? It depends on the company and the products themselves. Not all sounds are created equal, and there are many variables that contribute to a sound's quality. As of this writing, the sounds of the trumpet, saxophone, oboe, and individual string instruments (such as violin and viola) are often poor. However, piano and other keyboard sounds such as the DX-7, Rhodes, and Hammond B-3 organ tend to be excellently rendered.

QUESTION?

What's the difference between analog and digital?
In analog, electronic wave forms are continuous and always changing. Also, the number of values is infinite. Digital technology uses distinct pulses to transmit, store, and process electronic information through a strict binary code of zeros and ones.

Synthesizers

Synthesizers are considered keyboard instruments since most of them use a standard keyboard layout to produce specific pitches and sound effects. Old fashioned synths make a sound by manipulating and controlling electronic voltage. For example, a variety of sounds can be created by manipulating the sine wave of an electronic tone. Classic analog synthesizers used operational amplifiers (op-amps) as well as potentiometers to change or modify the sound. They also used oscillators and filters to change the frequency or wavelength of a tone. The first synths were referred to as modular since they were a patchwork of independent electronic units.

Bob Moog

Contrary to myth, Bob Moog did not invent the synthesizer. However, he was the first to popularize this keyboard instrument. A brilliant engineer,

Moog invented the now-famous Minimoog (1970). This efficient, single unit synth quickly replaced the cumbersome, multiple units of the day. Like earlier synthesizers, the Minimoog was still monophonic, meaning it could only play one note at a time. However, it single-handedly revolutionized the world of keyboards.

More than anything, Moog's synthesizers spurred a greater interest in keyboard technology. By 1979, curiosity with synthetic and nonacoustic sound eventually led to Digital Signal Processing, which converts or manipulates analog information. And despite the advances of the digital age, some keyboardists still enjoy using the old Moog synths. Enthusiasts claim that their warm, analog sounds cannot be imitated by microprocessors or computers.

In 2006, Moog Music unveiled the Little Phatty Analog Synthesizer. A tribute to the late Bob Moog, this sleek keyboard includes all the classic Minimoog features but with a musical instrument digital interface (MIDI).

FACT

The full name of the piano is *pianoforte*. It was first invented around 1700 by an Italian named Bartolomeo Cristofori. The piano continued to evolve and change dramatically until the modern piano was born in the late 1800s.

Piano Versus Keyboard

When choosing a piano or a keyboard, you will need to consider many variables. A casual search using your browser will reveal many retail outlets and many brand names. With so much information available, and so many products to choose from, you will need to keep your musical objectives in mind. In the end, it all boils down to two main questions:

- What will best serve my musical goals?
- What can I realistically afford?

For most students, the answer is to purchase a digital keyboard. Pianos can be quite a financial investment, or even a financial burden. Plus, they are not portable and they don't offer a wide range of sounds. The old blues and rock players used pianos because the keyboard hadn't been invented. However, by the 1960s, early electric keyboards became popular for the very same reasons listed earlier: mobility and sound selection.

Today, keyboard technology offers many new alternatives. In the 1960s, no one could have imagined how good the digital (sampled) organ and piano sounds could become, or how easy it could be to hook your keyboard up to your computer to create stunning home recordings. With a simple MIDI hookup and the appropriate computer software, you can now record music in your apartment or create lengthy musical scores without the use of pen and ink.

QUESTION?

Should I own both a piano and a keyboard?
There is no need to own both. If you're a beginner, don't spend your money on an expensive piano unless you truly have the money to spare. Instead, buy a keyboard with fully weighted or semi-weighted keys. Also purchase a practice amplifier, a quarter-inch instrument cable, and an adjustable keyboard bench (or drum throne).

Nonetheless, the acoustic piano still has a worthy and distinguished place in our society, and students with slightly more means and space still enjoy tickling on the ole ivories. In fact, upright and spinet pianos remain popular with families who like to gather round and sing songs together. Often, these pianos are handed down from generation to generation, and they help to keep nuclear and extended families connected.

It would be unwise to quote specific prices in this book since prices fluctuate constantly. As implied earlier, pianos are generally more expensive than keyboards. If you plan on purchasing a keyboard, you may be able to get something of quality for under a thousand dollars. A keen researcher might also find a decent upright piano in this same price bracket, but this is increasingly rare.

Top piano brands like Steinway & Sons, Yamaha, Baldwin, Kawai, or Bosendorfer can get very expensive for middle-class incomes. Grand and baby grand pianos from these companies can range from $25,000 to $200,000! There are cheaper, second-rate piano companies, but their pianos often have a shorter lifespan.

Buying the Right Piano

Buying a piano is a big step and an indication that you're serious about your music. Upright pianos remain the most cost-effective although they don't sound as full or magnificent as a baby grand or grand. The advantage is that uprights take up less room in your house. No matter what kind of piano you buy, new and used pianos from reputable merchants will usually serve you well. Still, it is best to watch out for fast-talking salespeople who may be looking to make a hefty commission off of you.

When browsing in any piano showroom, make sure that you come prepared. This means telling sellers that you have sought and will continue to seek the advice of a registered piano technician. This will help you get a fairer price since you are also less likely to get pigeonholed as an ignorant buyer. For quick reference on techs, be sure to visit the Piano Technicians Guild Web site listed in Appendix B. There you will find invaluable advice on technicians plus information on how to care for, maintain, and service your piano.

Don't forget to have your piano tuned regularly. You should tune your piano two to four times annually. More than anything, humidity causes the wood to contract and expand with the weather. Hygrometers can help you monitor the relative humidity in your home. You can also purchase humidity control devices for pianos.

You need to be especially cautious when purchasing a used piano from the guy down the street. If you read an advertisement in the classifieds section of your local newspaper that uses the words *a deal*, or even worse, *a steal*, you need to be particularly vigilant. People try to sell unusable, unplayable pianos all the time. Again, the first step is to seek the advice of a registered piano technician. But don't just rely on his or her expertise. Educate yourself as much as possible about what to look for in a quality instrument.

Broken keys, bent hammers, worn-out felt, cracked sounding boards, rickety lyres, and even fractured plates (cast-iron piano frame) are all signs of a piano in disrepair. When examining a piano, of any kind, look and listen for these three signature problems:

- Worn felt on hammers
- Cracked sounding board or ribs on sounding board that have become unglued
- Rotting wooden pinblock

If the felt on the hammers is totally worn away, the piano is a goner. Replacing the hammers can be very cost prohibitive. If the sounding board is cracked, the piano will buzz and hum when played. Again, this is a very expensive repair. Finally, if the wooden pinblock is in disrepair, the piano will not stay in tune, so it won't be worth a dime to you. Broken keys can be fixed without breaking the bank, but often these sunken keys reveal additional problems lurking inside.

There are many other mechanical problems that can diminish the value of a piano, but these issues are particularly ominous. Remember, too, that purchasing a piano from an individual seller will mean that no warranty will be attached to the sale. For this reason alone, it is probably best to stick with reputable dealers.

Buying the Right Keyboard

Keyboards are less of a financial investment, but that doesn't mean that they're all easy on the pocket. They can get pricey: around $3,000 or more. However, there are many good options in a much lower price range. Keyboards are also easier to maintain. No piano tuners are required and the care and maintenance of a keyboard is undemanding. For example, keyboards are not as susceptible to weather (humidity). However, you need to make sure your keyboard doesn't get wet. Water is the enemy to electrical components. Also, if you drop your keyboard, the electronics could become damaged, so buy a carrying case.

Shopping for a keyboard can become a daunting task, since there are so many varieties out there. It's hard to know where to start. This chapter has stressed needs above anything else. As with pianos, you will have to consider what your musical goals or objectives are before purchasing a keyboard. If you're interested in mimicking a piano for old-time rock-n-roll or boogie-woogie, buy a simple digital piano. In this case, you might as well go the whole nine yards and get a weighted-action, eighty-eight-key instrument. Kurzweil, Roland, Yamaha, and Korg all make good digital stage pianos. Whatever you buy, just make sure that your keyboard is MIDI capable and velocity sensitive.

Velocity sensitivity or touch sensitivity is a must. Velocity sensitivity refers to dynamic range. In other words, the harder you strike a note, the louder it sounds. Velocity sensitivity should not be confused with aftertouch or pressure sensitivity, which triggers a controller to alter the actual sound or pitch.

If you're interested in contemporary, techno-driven music, and modern keyboard applications, you may want to buy a digital workstation. A workstation is a one-stop shop for all your techno indulgences. You've heard about the kid in the candy store? The workstation is the keyboardist's equivalent.

If you know how to operate all the bells and whistles found on today's keyboards, then workstations are a good option for you. They are usually paired with digital synthesizers and offer features such as sampling, mixing, editing, sequencing, hard disc audio recording, CD burning, and more. Each year, up-to-the-minute expanded models hit the showroom floors, and the technological innovations just keep on coming. The trend has always been to create keyboards that are not only user friendly but also artistically stimulating. The more sounds, presets, and creativity features a company can offer, the better their product will sell. Companies such as Alesis and Yamaha know this, so the technology just keeps getting better and better.

The Benefits of Synths and Workstations

Digital synth technology allows for something called "virtual analog" and massive, multi-voice polyphony. The old synths were always monophonic, meaning that only one note could be played at a time. Digital technology has now left monophony in the dust and now more than a hundred voices can sound at once.

Sequencing features also include arpeggio presets for the technically challenged keyboardist. If you recall Chapter 8, you will remember that arpeggios are staggered chord tones. (When playing an arpeggio, each note is played independently and in succession.) Finally, digital synths offer a plethora of effects, including reverbs, choruses, and equalizers (EQ). Like their predecessors, they also all have pitch bend and modulation wheels, which further alter and transform notes. What does all this jargon and technical talk mean? Let's just say that it all adds up to a wide palette of sounds and tone colors. Ultimately, this allows for more artistic and creative freedom.

The Pitfalls of Synths and Workstations

The only pitfall is that many use "synth touch" rather than "piano action." If you're a student of the piano, you may find the light, nonweighted keys of a synthesizer to be foreign and even problematic. On the other hand, some keyboardists believe that they play faster using synth touch, so it all comes down to your personal preference.

Further, some workstations do not have eighty-eight keys like a piano. For example, you may come across sixty-one-note synthesizers or keyboards with even fewer keys. This can be a drawback for some performers who enjoy using the lowest and highest octaves of a piano. Lastly, if you're not particularly technically savvy, you can be easily confused by synths, workstations, and all the glitz that surrounds keyboard technology. Any way you dice it, keyboards have become a veritable playground of gizmos and gadgetry. But if you're up for the challenge, many incredible musical adventures await you. In the next chapter, we will expand on our discussion of equipment to talk about learning tools and technology.

Chapter 17

Accessories and Learning Tools

New tools, gadgets, and software are being developed every year. While new does not always mean better, there are many products on the market that really do help you get more out of the experience of music making. Since technology is always changing and updating, this chapter will not go into detail about the latest trends. Instead, it will give you a general idea of the tools and accessories that are likely to grow, develop, and remain vital.

The Metronome

Metronomes are pulsating devises that aid in the development of time and rhythm. A metronome is a compact, plastic box that creates an electronic beeping sound. This beep or click is sometimes accompanied by a flashing light. The beeps and the lights are designed to help you maintain a steady beat. When used properly, metronomes help you develop a keen internal clock.

There are many brands of metronomes on the market and prices range from a few bucks to well over a hundred dollars. Some of these companies include Seiko, Wittner, Korg, Qwik Time, Yamaha, Franz, Exacto, and Boss. You can now also download click tracks from the Internet. Additionally, drum machines can serve as fancy metronomes. For example, you might enjoy playing along with a drum groove rather than a click.

The best metronomes on the market are ones that can really be turned up and ones that come with an earphone jack. Pocket metronomes have little use for the piano since they are not loud enough. The classic Dr. Beat DB-66 metronome (by Boss) and its newer counterpart the Dr. Beat DB-90 metronomes are the best on the market.

ALERT!

Whatever metronome you use, stay far away from manual, windup, or pendulum metronomes. These are obsolete, and their timekeeping is dubious. Questionable time on a metronome defeats the purpose of even using one. In fact, it may actually hurt your playing. Stick with Quartz metronomes since they have perfect time even as the battery fades.

The Dr. Beat DB-66 metronome offers many features, including a dual light. One light is designated for beat one only; the second light pulsates on the remaining beats in the measure. In 4/4, beat one blinks on the left side of the metronome while beats two, three, and four blink on the right side of the metronome. The Dr. Beat can also play multiple rhythms. In other words, you can add eighth notes, sixteenth notes, or triplets to the mix simply by turning up the volume on the individual sliders. Furthermore, the Dr. Beat offers a wide range of tempo and meter choices, and it features a tap function. The tap function allows you to set the tempo by tapping the speed you desire. A digital readout will tell you what tempo you are tapping. You can then set the metronome accordingly. To save on the cost of batteries, the Dr. Beat also comes with an AC adapter.

Setting the Metronome

There are many ways to set a metronome. If you're in 4/4, for example, you may want to set the metronome to represent all four downbeats. However, as the tempo increases, you may find it helpful to set the metronome to represent half notes. If you're having trouble playing with the metronome, set it so that it represents eighth notes or even sixteenth notes. Note divisions and subdivisions will help you play with greater rhythmical accuracy. Also, don't forget to set the metronome so that the clicks and lights fit the meter or time signature you're playing in. The loudest click should always represent beat one.

FACT

If you set the metronome to sixty, there will be sixty clicks played per minute. In other words, the metronome will be clicking seconds. Obviously, higher numbers mean more clicks per minute, while lower numbers mean fewer clicks per minute.

Sometimes students set the metronome and then ignore it as they play. Don't fall into this trap! The metronome must click in sync with your rhythms. Otherwise, it's serving no purpose. If you have a difficult time playing in sync with the metronome, don't stress. You'll get it. That's what practice is for. However, don't just ignore it. **FIGURE 17-1** shows you a series of rhythms in 4/4 with metronome pulses indicated above the staff. In this time signature, the metronome is usually set to play quarter notes. Notice how the quarter notes line up with the downbeats of each rhythm.

Tap the rhythms to **FIGURE 17-1** slowly on your lap. You may also clap them if the tempo is not too fast. Also, make sure you count the rhythms out loud

FIGURE 17-1:

Playing with a
Metronome

as you tap. You will tap more accurately when you count aloud. Syncing up with a metronome requires patience and perseverance. However, if you keep at it, you will learn how to play at a steady, even pace.

Gauging Your Progress

When practicing a piece of music, start by setting the metronome at a moderate speed. If the piece still feels fast, decrease the tempo even more. If it's too slow, increase the speed in gradual increments until you find a comfortable start tempo or home base. You will perform best at moderately slow speeds. If you're playing too fast, you will not be able to meet the technical challenges of the piece. If you're playing too slow, you will find that you rush through all of the rhythms. Stick with "middle-of-the-road" tempos at first.

Once you find a relaxed, moderate start tempo, practice at this speed until you feel ready to move on. When you're ready to move on, increase the tempo one or two clicks; then try playing the piece again. If that feels good, try increasing the speed again until you reach the desired tempo. As you do this, you may want to keep a written log of the tempo increases you've made.

This log will be used to evaluate your progress. Over the course of many days, you will start to see a pattern emerge. If you're making improvement, you will notice that your tempos increase at a slow but steady rate. If you're attempting to play speeds that are beyond your ability, or if you haven't found a comfortable start tempo, this will be reflected in your metronome log. In this case, you will notice that your log shows erratic tempo shifts.

Each day, you may find that you have to back up from the previous day's top speed and then build from there. This is natural and it probably means that you just aren't warmed up yet. Also, sooner or later you will come up against a wall, and you will not be able to play any faster. This wall will represent your top speed on any given day. Finding your wall is a good thing. It allows you to set realistic and definite goals.

The goal is not always to play fast. Pianists must also be able to play slow, beautiful ballads. See how slowly you can play an exercise or a piece of music. You'll find that the slower you go, the harder it is to play accurate rhythms. This is because the slower you play, the more space there is between notes.

Practicing with a metronome can be frustrating, so you might be tempted to turn it off during your daily workout. Don't fall into this lazy trap. Also, some students mistrust metronomes, complaining that they keep bad time. Usually, the complaint is that the metronome is dragging. Do not buy into this myth. If you have a good metronome, it is always right. Developing the ability to play effortlessly with a metronome is a sign of skillful musicianship, so make this one of your priorities.

Music-Writing Software

With the development of the home computer and word-processing programs, printing presses and publishing houses lost their monopoly over print media. The same is true of musical notation. Now, you can format scores to look as clean and articulate as the published materials that come out of even the most advanced publishing houses: all in the comfort of your own living room.

No longer do you have to scribble notes by hand on staff paper or hire assistants to copy and transpose parts. Score-writing software such as Finale and Sibelius make it possible for musicians to format their music with the same kind of accuracy and professional appearance as a top-notch publishing house.

Both Finale and Sibelius contain score-writing or sheet music templates. With a click of the mouse, you can choose the staff paper of your liking. For example, you can select a piano staff, a four-piece jazz combo staff, or a modern orchestra staff. You can also customize your own score-writing templates. Once you choose your staff, you then select a key and time signature. You may also indicate tempo. After this, you begin inputting notes either through a keypad, keyboard shortcuts, or a MIDI hookup. When inputting notes through an interface, you simply play a keyboard, or other MIDI instrument, and the notes appear on the page. For example, much of the notation in this book was written using Sibelius's Flexi-time (real-time) input.

FACT

Transposition is the process of shifting from one key to another key. A piano is a nontransposing instrument. It plays in so-called "concert" pitch. However, some instruments, like the B-flat trumpet, are transposing instruments. When a B-flat trumpeter reads a middle C, she's really playing a concert B-flat.

MIDI technology is getting more and more advanced. However, at this stage, you still need to edit notes input through MIDI hookups so that a performer can read them without unnecessary complications. Sometimes the software accurately captures your music. Other times, it requires some manual editing. However, both Sibelius and Finale are rapidly becoming more "intelligent." Even at this stage, they make score writing infinitely faster than pen, ink, and paper.

One of the reasons for this is Sibelius's and Finale's ability to transpose music for you. They both also offer excellent sound libraries to play back your music. This helps you proofread with your ears as well as your eyes. No longer do you have to imagine what your score will sound like. With these playback features, you can now hear mistakes that your eyes might miss. Further, playback options are improving every year as sound samples evolve to include greater musical expression and nuance. There's no telling how far this software will evolve.

Band-in-a-Box

Band-in-a-Box is an excellent resource for students and professionals alike. This program is used to accompany a soloist. All you need to do is download the software onto your computer, type in some chords (harmony), choose a style of music to play, and begin improvising. When indicating chords, you can write simple triads or complex chords with all kinds of harmonic extensions (e.g., Cmin9#11). Band-in-a-Box does the rest for you. Depending on the style of music you choose, Band-in-a-Box will interpret the music and voice the chords appropriately. From jazz to rock, blues to Latin, Band-in-a-Box plays it all.

During playback, Band-in-a-Box can accompany you on an assortment of instruments. For example, you can play along with just a bass track or you can mix in a drum groove. If you want, you can also add guitar or piano chords, although this feature is designed more for horn players. You can even add a string arrangement to make your practice session really sound lush.

ALERT!

While Band-in-a-Box can help you streamline your ideas and gain confidence soloing in real time, nothing can match the experience of playing with actual human beings. Music is an interactive endeavor that involves sensitivity, compromise, unity, and cooperation. No music software can fully simulate the experience of performing with others.

Band-in-a-Box is especially helpful when learning how to improvise over the blues. Enter I, IV, and V chords (in the key of C major) into Band-in-a-Box. Once you've done this, practice soloing over these chords at different speeds. If you're more advanced, try soloing over jazz-blues chord changes. These include ii–V and iii, vi, ii, V, I chordal movements. Once you play with Band-in-a-Box, you will quickly find out what you're able to play and what you're not able to play. Like metronomes, Band-in-a-Box will keep you honest. This software plays with complete accuracy so you will know if you're dragging or rushing or if you're attempting a speed, or a piece of music for that matter, that is beyond your abilities.

Once you cut your teeth in C major, practice the blues in other keys. Professional pianists are expected to be masters of transposition. This book focuses on C major since it's easier to learn new concepts when playing in a key that does not use sharps or flats. However, you should learn blues licks and clichés in every key.

Are there favored keys? Yes. The most common blues keys are E, A, B-flat, and F major. Guitarists favor E and A major; horn players tend to favor B-flat and F major. These keys are favored because of the way these instruments are made. In other words, instrumentalists tend to play in keys that suit their instrument's construction. Pianists favor C since there are fewer accidentals. However, it is expected that you can play in all fifteen keys. If anything, keys with five to seven sharps/flats are less common and therefore less important. However, you shouldn't ignore these keys altogether.

More than anything, Band-in-a-Box will help you discover your strengths and weaknesses. You will also get a taste of what it's like to play with musicians. However, bear in mind that real musicians are not machines that play as perfectly and smoothly as Band-in-a-Box. Consequently, it's important to get out there and play with real people, too.

Home Recording

One aspect of music making that has made dramatic changes over the last twenty-five years is home recording. In fact, no longer do you need to pay high prices at recording studios to create first-rate recordings. Prior to the digital age, most home recording was done on multitrack cassette decks. Tascam's Portastudio was especially popular in the early 1980s. These devices allowed people to record up to eight tracks, but the sound quality could not compete with the two-inch tape, reel-to-reel, and console setups found in professional studios.

By the mid 1980s, Digital Audio Tape (DAT) recorders became a viable home recording option, but this was limited to recording "live to two-track." In 1991, the Alesis Digital Audio Tape (ADAT) was introduced and this allowed enthusiasts to record up to eight tracks onto Super VHS magnetic tape. Despite the promise of this technology, home-recording buffs still needed to "bounce" tracks down, or synchronize machines together, if they wanted to record more than eight tracks.

If you're new to home recording, try GarageBand, a user-friendly program from Apple Computer. GarageBand allows you to build loops from their collection of instrument samples. You can also record your own instruments by using an interface or a microphone. With easy editing options, GarageBand is a good primer for home recording.

Today, home computers are used to create recordings with stunning clarity and resolution, and there are virtually no limits to the amount of tracks you can use. If you have good ears, reasonable computer skills, ample workspace, and a lot of patience, you can record your tunes in the comfort of your own home. To get started, all you need is a Mac or a personal computer and a Digital Audio Workstation (DAW) such as Pro Tools, Nuendo, Cubase, Logic, Digital Performer, or Sonar. Next, you need an interface and an array of quality plug-ins (reverbs, compressors, and equalizers). If you plan on recording acoustic or "live" instruments, you will also need some quality microphones. Once you know how to use this technology, you can engineer and produce your own music. If you pay attention to detail, your music can rival recordings made in professional studios. Check out *The Everything*® *Home Recording Book* for more information.

Recording Music for Educational Purposes

You should get to know current technology so that you can "enter into the game" and have others hear your music. But this isn't the only reason to record your playing. Recording and documenting your work is good for your budding career, and it's extremely educational.

Past generations of music students had few opportunities to record and document their progress. This is far from the truth today. If you possess recorded documents of each stage in your musical development, you will get better at a faster rate. How? If you record yourself regularly, you can better measure your progress.

Through recordings, you can listen to your performance(s) after the fact and you can be your own teacher. Once you remove yourself from the mechanics of music making, you will be able to listen with a more objective ear. In other words, you will be able to hear yourself as others hear you. This is an invaluable tool, especially if you do not take private lessons. It's hard to critique your playing in the heat of the moment. However, if you can go back and listen to what you played, you will be able to evaluate your music more truthfully. You will be able to determine if you are keeping steady time and playing clean, confident rhythms. When listening to recordings of yourself, listen for tone and expression, melody, harmony, improvisation, and of course, to hear if you are playing the correct notes.

Tone and Expression

While listening, ask yourself, "Am I creating an attractive, euphonious, and expressive sound on the piano?" If not, think about how you're striking the keys. Consider revamping your technique and posture if necessary (see Chapter 2). Regarding expression, think about how you're creating phrases on the piano. Phrases are similar to sentence structure. Don't create the equivalent of run-on sentences when you play. All music must have distinct beginnings and ends just like sentences. Also, don't play mono-dynamically. Your phrases should generally arc (crescendo and decrescendo) as they move from beginning to end. Adding accents is another way to add excitement to your phrases.

Melody

Are you creating compelling melodies? Can you hum what you're playing? Are you building off a motif(s), or are you wandering randomly up and down the keyboard? If you're unhappy with your melodicism, listen to more music. The best way to develop a strong sense of melody is to experience the splendor of other people's melodies. Check out a wide variety of music to see how melody interacts with harmony, rhythm, and song structure. Also, don't be afraid to use repetition and "theme and variation" in your melodies.

Harmony

Are your chords complementing or clashing with the melody? Can you use more colorful or expressive chords? "Accompanist" is practically the pianist's middle name. More than anything else, pianists are required to be able to back up singers and soloists well. If your harmonic sense is weak, you'll be limited in your ability to find work as a pianist. This applies to virtually any style of music. Therefore, focus on developing an immaculate sense of harmony and counterpoint. On this instrument, harmonic abilities separate the boys from the men and the girls from the women. If you're looking for review, harmony is formally introduced in Chapter 6.

Improvisation

There is nothing worse than sketchy improvisation. While listening to your recording, ask yourself, "Am I able to play meaningful solos? What about my note choice? Do I make lots of errors when I solo, or do I play licks that fit well over the given chord changes?" All students of piano play some wonky notes. That's okay. Everybody plays questionable solos at first. It's all part of the learning process. If you're playing a lot of "clams," as musicians call them, go back and think about how chords interact with scales and modes. Perhaps you are playing too many "avoid" notes when using a particular scale over a chord. Or perhaps you are using the wrong modes altogether.

Wrong Notes

Obviously, you should use your ear to discriminate between right and wrong notes. However, if you're a novice, you won't detect every wrong note. Therefore, you must judiciously review scale and chord theory to ensure proper note choices. Additionally, don't forget to listen to recordings by professional pianists. Listening will help your ear gradually discern right and wrong notes. Wrong notes do exist. There is a difference between dissonant note choices and wrong note choices. If you're careful and meticulous in your study of music, you will gradually learn how to play solos that impress listeners and musicians alike.

Appendix A

Key Innovators and Recordings

Here is a list of essential rock, pop, blues, and jazz-blues pianists/keyboardist together with one or two of their finer albums. This list is by no means exhaustive; it's more of a point of departure. Note: If the pianist or keyboardist is not the leader, the artist or band name will be listed in parentheses.

Rock, Pop, and Electric Keyboard

Elton John—*Captain Fantastic and the Brown Dirt Cowboy* and *Sleeping with the Past*

Billy Joel—*The Nylon Curtain* and *12 Gardens Live*

Donald Fagen—*The Nightfly*

Bruce Hornsby—*Harbor Lights*

Jon Lord—*Machine Head* (Deep Purple)

Rick Wakeman—*Close to the Edge* (Yes) and *Journey to the Centre of the Earth*

Tony Banks—*Selling England by the Pound* (Genesis)

Keith Emerson—*Emerson, Lake & Palmer* and *Brain Salad Surgery* (ELP)

Richard Wright—*Dark Side of the Moon* (Pink Floyd)

Kraftwerk—*Autobahn* and *Minimum–Maximum*

Gary Numan—*Telekon*

Brian Eno—*Ambient 1: Music for Airports*

Nicky Hopkins—*Tin Man Was a Dreamer*

Patrick Moraz—*Relayer* (Yes)

Joe Jackson—*Night & Day* and *Afterlife*

Kenny Kirkland—*Dream of the Blue Turtles* (Sting)

Ben Folds—*Ben Folds Five*

Tori Amos—*Little Earthquakes*

Randy Newman—*Sail Away* and *Bad Love*

R&B, Early Rock-n-Roll, and Soul
Fats Domino—*Early Imperial Singles 1950–1952* and *The Imperial Singles, Volumes 2 and 3*

Ray Charles—*Pure Genius: The Complete Atlantic Recordings (1952–1959)* and *Strong Love Affair*

Little Richard—*Here's Little Richard* and *The Fabulous Little Richard*

Jerry Lee Lewis—*Jerry Lee Lewis* and *The Return of Rock*

Art Neville—*Art Neville: His Specialty Recordings 1956–1958* and *Yellow Moon* (The Neville Brothers)

Johnnie Johnson—*Johnnie B. Bad*

Stevie Wonder—*Innervisions* and *Original Musiquarium I*

Jools Holland—*Friends 3*

Billy Preston—*A Whole New Thing*

Blues and Jazz
Charles Brown—*Black Night*

Jay McShann—*Hootie Blues* and *Goin' to Kansas City*

Nat King Cole—*Hit That Jive: 1936–1946* (Nat King Cole Trio) and *The Very Best of Nat King Cole*

Pete Johnson—*Pete's Blues*

Jimmy Yancey and Pete Johnson—*Jazz Piano Masters: Jimmy Yancey* and *Jazz Piano Masters: Pete Johnson*

Meade "Lux" Lewis—*The Blues Piano Artistry of Meade Lux Lewis*

Albert Ammons—*Boogie Woogie Stomp*

Charles "Cow Cow" Davenport—*Complete Recorded Works, Vol. 2 (1929–1945)*

Fats Waller—*Handful of Keys*

James P. Johnson—*Snowy Morning Blues*

Willie "The Lion" Smith—*Pork and Beans*

Count Basie—*For the Second Time* (Count Basie and the Kansas City 3) and *Straight Ahead*

Duke Ellington—*Piano Reflections* and *Three Suites*

Thelonious Monk—*Straight, No Chaser* and *Monk's Dream*

Brother Jack McDuff—*Moon Rappin'*

Jimmy Smith—*The Cat*

Dorothy Donegan—*The Explosive Dorothy Donegan*

Marcia Ball—*Gatorrhythms*

Jelly Roll Morton—*Birth of the Hot*

Harry Connick Jr.—*Occasion: Connick on Piano, Vol. 2*

Dr. John—*Goin' Back to New Orleans* and *Right Place, Right Time: Live at Tipitina's*

Allan Toussaint—*The Wild Sound of New Orleans: The Complete 'Tousan' Sessions*

Professor Longhair—*Crawfish Fiesta*

Champion Jack Dupree—*Blues from the Gutter*

James Booker—*New Orleans Piano Wizard: Live!*

Otis Spann—*Otis Spann Is the Blues* and *The Bottom of the Blues*

Sunnyland Slim—*Midnight Jump*

Willie "Pinetop" Perkins—*Down in Mississippi* and *Heritage of the Blues: The Complete Hightone Sessions*

Roosevelt Sykes—*Hard Drivin' Blues*

Peetie Wheatstraw—*The Last Straw*

Blues Compilations

Various Artists—*Essential Blues Piano*

Various Artists—*Martin Scorsese Presents the Blues: Piano Blues*

Various Artists—*A Celebration of Blues: Great Blues Piano*

Appendix B

Resources

Here is a list of books, Internet sites, and films/videos that will help you learn more about rock and blues as discussed in this book. Again, this list is by no means exhaustive. It is meant to serve as a springboard for your own research.

Publications

Beatlemania 1963 to 1966 Volume I and *Beatlemania 1967–1970 Volume II* (Hal Leonard Corporation, 1986).

Bogdanov, Vladimir, Chris Woodstra, and Stephen Thomas Erlewine. *All Music Guide to the Blues: The Definitive Guide to the Blues* (Backbeat Books, 2003).

Chords for Keyboard and Guitar: Pocket Reference Guide to More Than 1800 Chords (Hal Leonard Corporation, 1995).

Finn, Julio. *The Bluesman: The Musical Heritage of Black Men and Women in the Americas* (Interlink Books, 1991).

Hanon, C. L. *Hanon: The Virtuoso Pianist in Sixty Exercises for the Piano* (G. Schirmer's, Inc., 1928).

Harrison, Mark. *Blues Piano: The Complete Guide with CD* (Hal Leonard Corporation, 2003).

Kriss, Eric. *Beginning Blues Piano* (Amsco Publications, 1984).

Manzarek, Ray. *Light My Fire: My Life with the Doors* (Berkeley Boulevard, 1998).

Ostwald, Andy. *Play Jazz, Blues, & Rock Piano by Ear, Book One* (Mel Bay, 2003).

Palmer, Robert. *Deep Blues* (Penguin Books, 1981).

Rebennack, Mac (Dr. John) and Jack Rummel. *Under a Hoodoo Moon: The Life of Dr. John the Night Tripper* (St. Martin's Press, 1994).

Schonbrun, Marc. *The Everything® Reading Music Book* (Adams Media, 2005).

Helpful Music Web Sites

✏ *www.allmusic.com*
✏ *www.blues.org*
✏ *www.cdbaby.com*
✏ *www.garageband.com*
✏ *www.ptg.org*
✏ *www.pianoeducation.org*
✏ *www.piano.com*
✏ *www.pianoworld.com*
✏ *www.rockhall.com*
✏ *www.steinway.com*
✏ *www.vh1.com*
✏ *www.wikipedia.com*

Film/DVD

Learn to Play Blues Piano #1: A Beginner's Guide to Improvisation by David Bennett Cohen (Homespun Video)

Learning Rock-n-Roll Piano (Homespun Video)

Martin Scorsese Presents the Blues: Piano Blues (Sony Video)

Piano Grand! A Smithsonian Celebration by Various Artists (Sony Video)

The Blues/Rock Piano of Johnnie Johnson: Sessions with a Keyboard Legend (Homespun Video)

The Piano Styles of Dr. John: An Intimate Session with Mac Rebennack (Homespun Video)

Index

Oral tradition, 2–3
Ostinato, 125
Outros, 174

Parallel key, 77
Parker, Charlie, 4, 152, 158
Pedals, 46–48
Pentatonic scales, 56–58, 107–10
Perfect fourth intervals, 59
Perkins, Pinetop, 7, 152
Phillips, Sam, 6–7
Phrases, 135–36
Piano
    about, 242–43, 245
    buying, 247–48
    fingering, 21–22
    hand and finger placement, 20–21
    keyboard layout, 12–18
    vs. keyboards, 242, 245–47
    overview of, 11–22
    pedals, 46–48
    sitting at, 18–19
Piano pop, 213–16
Piano rock, 9
Piedmont blues, 155–56
Pitch, 12, 25–26
Pop, 170, 181, 184, 212–13
Powell, Billy, 211, 212
Powell, Bud, 161
Presley, Elvis, 7
Progressive rock, 206–8

Quarter notes, 32

Ragtime, 4
Range, 24–25
Rap, 9
Recording, 258–61
Record labels, 5, 7, 155
Refrain, 174
Repetition, 136–37
Rests, 24, 30
Rhythm, 28–30
Rhythm and blues (R&B), 184
Riffs, 132–34
Rock
    dawning of era of, 184
    development of, 201–16
    distinguishing from pop, 170
    elements of, 169–82
    history of, 6–7
    progressive, 206–8
    Southern, 209–12
    styles of, 9–10
Roxy Music, 212
Rubato, 34

Sampling technology, 8
Scalar exercises, 49–52
Scale degrees, 16–18
Scales
    blues, 54–55, 111–12, 132
    combining chords with, 100–114
    dominant, 61–64, 112–14
    Dorian mode, 58–60, 105–7

Lydian dominant, 64–66, 112–14
    major, 38–42, 58, 69–70
    minor, 42–46, 101–2
    Mixolydian mode, 60–61
    pentatonic, 56–58, 107–10
Secondary dominant chords, 76–77
Sharps, 36–37
Shell voicings, 72
Shuffle, 123–24
Singer-songwriters, 213–16
Sixth intervals, 165
Slavery, 3–4
Sloan, Henry, 4
Smith, Willie "The Lion," 6
"Solar Wind for Polyphonic Synthesizer," 228, 231–35
Soloing, 101–14
Solo sections, 174
Song forms, 173–75
Sostenuto pedal, 46–47
Southern rock, 211
Spirituals, 3–4
Staff, 24
Steps, 14–15
St. Louis blues, 6, 157
Stoller, Mike, 6–7
Stride, 160
Structural elements, of songs, 174–75
Study pieces, 217–39
Sun Records, 7
Suspended chords, 89–92
Sustain pedal, 46–48

THE EVERYTHING SERIES!

BUSINESS & PERSONAL FINANCE

Everything® Accounting Book
Everything® Budgeting Book
Everything® Business Planning Book
Everything® Coaching and Mentoring Book
Everything® Fundraising Book
Everything® Get Out of Debt Book
Everything® Grant Writing Book
Everything® Guide to Personal Finance for Single Mothers
Everything® Home-Based Business Book, 2nd Ed.
Everything® Homebuying Book, 2nd Ed.
Everything® Homeselling Book, 2nd Ed.
Everything® Improve Your Credit Book
Everything® Investing Book, 2nd Ed.
Everything® Landlording Book
Everything® Leadership Book
Everything® Managing People Book, 2nd Ed.
Everything® Negotiating Book
Everything® Online Auctions Book
Everything® Online Business Book
Everything® Personal Finance Book
Everything® Personal Finance in Your 20s and 30s Book
Everything® Project Management Book
Everything® Real Estate Investing Book
Everything® Retirement Planning Book
Everything® Robert's Rules Book, $7.95
Everything® Selling Book
Everything® Start Your Own Business Book, 2nd Ed.
Everything® Wills & Estate Planning Book

COOKING

Everything® Barbecue Cookbook
Everything® Bartender's Book, $9.95
Everything® Cheese Book
Everything® Chinese Cookbook
Everything® Classic Recipes Book
Everything® Cocktail Parties and Drinks Book
Everything® College Cookbook
Everything® Cooking for Baby and Toddler Book
Everything® Cooking for Two Cookbook
Everything® Diabetes Cookbook
Everything® Easy Gourmet Cookbook
Everything® Fondue Cookbook
Everything® Fondue Party Book
Everything® Gluten-Free Cookbook
Everything® Glycemic Index Cookbook
Everything® Grilling Cookbook

Everything® Healthy Meals in Minutes Cookbook
Everything® Holiday Cookbook
Everything® Indian Cookbook
Everything® Italian Cookbook
Everything® Low-Carb Cookbook
Everything® Low-Fat High-Flavor Cookbook
Everything® Low-Salt Cookbook
Everything® Meals for a Month Cookbook
Everything® Mediterranean Cookbook
Everything® Mexican Cookbook
Everything® No Trans Fat Cookbook
Everything® One-Pot Cookbook
Everything® Pizza Cookbook
Everything® Quick and Easy 30-Minute, 5-Ingredient Cookbook
Everything® Quick Meals Cookbook
Everything® Slow Cooker Cookbook
Everything® Slow Cooking for a Crowd Cookbook
Everything® Soup Cookbook
Everything® Stir-Fry Cookbook
Everything® Tex-Mex Cookbook
Everything® Thai Cookbook
Everything® Vegetarian Cookbook
Everything® Wild Game Cookbook
Everything® Wine Book, 2nd Ed.

GAMES

Everything® 15-Minute Sudoku Book, $9.95
Everything® 30-Minute Sudoku Book, $9.95
Everything® Blackjack Strategy Book
Everything® Brain Strain Book, $9.95
Everything® Bridge Book
Everything® Card Games Book
Everything® Card Tricks Book, $9.95
Everything® Casino Gambling Book, 2nd Ed.
Everything® Chess Basics Book
Everything® Craps Strategy Book
Everything® Crossword and Puzzle Book
Everything® Crossword Challenge Book
Everything® Crosswords for the Beach Book, $9.95
Everything® Cryptograms Book, $9.95
Everything® Easy Crosswords Book
Everything® Easy Kakuro Book, $9.95
Everything® Easy Large Print Crosswords Book
Everything® Games Book, 2nd Ed.
Everything® Giant Sudoku Book, $9.95
Everything® Kakuro Challenge Book, $9.95
Everything® Large-Print Crossword Challenge Book

Everything® Large-Print Crosswords Book
Everything® Lateral Thinking Puzzles Book, $9.95
Everything® Mazes Book
Everything® Movie Crosswords Book, $9.95
Everything® Online Poker Book, $12.95
Everything® Pencil Puzzles Book, $9.95
Everything® Poker Strategy Book
Everything® Pool & Billiards Book
Everything® Sports Crosswords Book, $9.95
Everything® Test Your IQ Book, $9.95
Everything® Texas Hold 'Em Book, $9.95
Everything® Travel Crosswords Book, $9.95
Everything® Word Games Challenge Book
Everything® Word Scramble Book
Everything® Word Search Book

HEALTH

Everything® Alzheimer's Book
Everything® Diabetes Book
Everything® Health Guide to Adult Bipolar Disorder
Everything® Health Guide to Controlling Anxiety
Everything® Health Guide to Fibromyalgia
Everything® Health Guide to Postpartum Care
Everything® Health Guide to Thyroid Disease
Everything® Hypnosis Book
Everything® Low Cholesterol Book
Everything® Massage Book
Everything® Menopause Book
Everything® Nutrition Book
Everything® Reflexology Book
Everything® Stress Management Book

HISTORY

Everything® American Government Book
Everything® American History Book, 2nd Ed.
Everything® Civil War Book
Everything® Freemasons Book
Everything® Irish History & Heritage Book
Everything® Middle East Book

HOBBIES

Everything® Candlemaking Book
Everything® Cartooning Book
Everything® Coin Collecting Book
Everything® Drawing Book
Everything® Family Tree Book, 2nd Ed.
Everything® Knitting Book
Everything® Knots Book
Everything® Photography Book

Everything® Quilting Book
Everything® Scrapbooking Book
Everything® Sewing Book
Everything® Soapmaking Book, 2nd Ed.
Everything® Woodworking Book

HOME IMPROVEMENT

Everything® Feng Shui Book
Everything® Feng Shui Decluttering Book, $9.95
Everything® Fix-It Book
Everything® Home Decorating Book
Everything® Home Storage Solutions Book
Everything® Homebuilding Book
Everything® Organize Your Home Book

KIDS' BOOKS

All titles are $7.95
Everything® Kids' Animal Puzzle & Activity Book
Everything® Kids' Baseball Book, 4th Ed.
Everything® Kids' Bible Trivia Book
Everything® Kids' Bugs Book
Everything® Kids' Cars and Trucks Puzzle & Activity Book
Everything® Kids' Christmas Puzzle & Activity Book
Everything® Kids' Cookbook
Everything® Kids' Crazy Puzzles Book
Everything® Kids' Dinosaurs Book
Everything® Kids' First Spanish Puzzle and Activity Book
Everything® Kids' Gross Cookbook
Everything® Kids' Gross Hidden Pictures Book
Everything® Kids' Gross Jokes Book
Everything® Kids' Gross Mazes Book
Everything® Kids' Gross Puzzle and Activity Book
Everything® Kids' Halloween Puzzle & Activity Book
Everything® Kids' Hidden Pictures Book
Everything® Kids' Horses Book
Everything® Kids' Joke Book
Everything® Kids' Knock Knock Book
Everything® Kids' Learning Spanish Book
Everything® Kids' Math Puzzles Book
Everything® Kids' Mazes Book
Everything® Kids' Money Book
Everything® Kids' Nature Book
Everything® Kids' Pirates Puzzle and Activity Book
Everything® Kids' Presidents Book
Everything® Kids' Princess Puzzle and Activity Book
Everything® Kids' Puzzle Book
Everything® Kids' Riddles & Brain Teasers Book
Everything® Kids' Science Experiments Book
Everything® Kids' Sharks Book
Everything® Kids' Soccer Book
Everything® Kids' States Book
Everything® Kids' Travel Activity Book

KIDS' STORY BOOKS

Everything® Fairy Tales Book

LANGUAGE

Everything® Conversational Japanese Book with CD, $19.95
Everything® French Grammar Book
Everything® French Phrase Book, $9.95
Everything® French Verb Book, $9.95
Everything® German Practice Book with CD, $19.95
Everything® Inglés Book
Everything® Intermediate Spanish Book with CD, $19.95
Everything® Learning Brazilian Portuguese Book with CD, $19.95
Everything® Learning French Book
Everything® Learning German Book
Everything® Learning Italian Book
Everything® Learning Latin Book
Everything® Learning Spanish Book with CD, 2nd Edition, $19.95
Everything® Russian Practice Book with CD, $19.95
Everything® Sign Language Book
Everything® Spanish Grammar Book
Everything® Spanish Phrase Book, $9.95
Everything® Spanish Practice Book with CD, $19.95
Everything® Spanish Verb Book, $9.95
Everything® Speaking Mandarin Chinese Book with CD, $19.95

MUSIC

Everything® Drums Book with CD, $19.95
Everything® Guitar Book with CD, 2nd Edition, $19.95
Everything® Guitar Chords Book with CD, $19.95
Everything® Home Recording Book
Everything® Music Theory Book with CD, $19.95
Everything® Reading Music Book with CD, $19.95
Everything® Rock & Blues Guitar Book with CD, $19.95
Everything® Rock and Blues Piano Book with CD, $19.95
Everything® Songwriting Book

NEW AGE

Everything® Astrology Book, 2nd Ed.
Everything® Birthday Personology Book
Everything® Dreams Book, 2nd Ed.
Everything® Love Signs Book, $9.95
Everything® Numerology Book
Everything® Paganism Book
Everything® Palmistry Book
Everything® Psychic Book
Everything® Reiki Book

Everything® Sex Signs Book, $9.95
Everything® Tarot Book, 2nd Ed.
Everything® Toltec Wisdom Book
Everything® Wicca and Witchcraft Book

PARENTING

Everything® Baby Names Book, 2nd Ed.
Everything® Baby Shower Book
Everything® Baby's First Year Book
Everything® Birthing Book
Everything® Breastfeeding Book
Everything® Father-to-Be Book
Everything® Father's First Year Book
Everything® Get Ready for Baby Book
Everything® Get Your Baby to Sleep Book, $9.95
Everything® Getting Pregnant Book
Everything® Guide to Raising a One-Year-Old
Everything® Guide to Raising a Two-Year-Old
Everything® Homeschooling Book
Everything® Mother's First Year Book
Everything® Parent's Guide to Childhood Illnesses
Everything® Parent's Guide to Children and Divorce
Everything® Parent's Guide to Children with ADD/ADHD
Everything® Parent's Guide to Children with Asperger's Syndrome
Everything® Parent's Guide to Children with Autism
Everything® Parent's Guide to Children with Bipolar Disorder
Everything® Parent's Guide to Children with Depression
Everything® Parent's Guide to Children with Dyslexia
Everything® Parent's Guide to Children with Juvenile Diabetes
Everything® Parent's Guide to Positive Discipline
Everything® Parent's Guide to Raising a Successful Child
Everything® Parent's Guide to Raising Boys
Everything® Parent's Guide to Raising Girls
Everything® Parent's Guide to Raising Siblings
Everything® Parent's Guide to Sensory Integration Disorder
Everything® Parent's Guide to Tantrums
Everything® Parent's Guide to the Strong-Willed Child
Everything® Parenting a Teenager Book
Everything® Potty Training Book, $9.95
Everything® Pregnancy Book, 3rd Ed.
Everything® Pregnancy Fitness Book
Everything® Pregnancy Nutrition Book
Everything® Pregnancy Organizer, 2nd Ed., $16.95
Everything® Toddler Activities Book
Everything® Toddler Book

Everything® Tween Book
Everything® Twins, Triplets, and More Book

PETS

Everything® Aquarium Book
Everything® Boxer Book
Everything® Cat Book, 2nd Ed.
Everything® Chihuahua Book
Everything® Dachshund Book
Everything® Dog Book
Everything® Dog Health Book
Everything® Dog Obedience Book
Everything® Dog Owner's Organizer, $16.95
Everything® Dog Training and Tricks Book
Everything® German Shepherd Book
Everything® Golden Retriever Book
Everything® Horse Book
Everything® Horse Care Book
Everything® Horseback Riding Book
Everything® Labrador Retriever Book
Everything® Poodle Book
Everything® Pug Book
Everything® Puppy Book
Everything® Rottweiler Book
Everything® Small Dogs Book
Everything® Tropical Fish Book
Everything® Yorkshire Terrier Book

REFERENCE

Everything® American Presidents Book
Everything® Blogging Book
Everything® Build Your Vocabulary Book
Everything® Car Care Book
Everything® Classical Mythology Book
Everything® Da Vinci Book
Everything® Divorce Book
Everything® Einstein Book
Everything® Enneagram Book
Everything® Etiquette Book, 2nd Ed.
Everything® Inventions and Patents Book
Everything® Mafia Book
Everything® Philosophy Book
Everything® Pirates Book
Everything® Psychology Book

RELIGION

Everything® Angels Book
Everything® Bible Book
Everything® Buddhism Book
Everything® Catholicism Book
Everything® Christianity Book
Everything® Gnostic Gospels Book
Everything® History of the Bible Book
Everything® Jesus Book

Everything® Jewish History & Heritage Book
Everything® Judaism Book
Everything® Kabbalah Book
Everything® Koran Book
Everything® Mary Book
Everything® Mary Magdalene Book
Everything® Prayer Book
Everything® Saints Book, 2nd Ed.
Everything® Torah Book
Everything® Understanding Islam Book
Everything® World's Religions Book
Everything® Zen Book

SCHOOL & CAREERS

Everything® Alternative Careers Book
Everything® Career Tests Book
Everything® College Major Test Book
Everything® College Survival Book, 2nd Ed.
Everything® Cover Letter Book, 2nd Ed.
Everything® Filmmaking Book
Everything® Get-a-Job Book, 2nd Ed.
Everything® Guide to Being a Paralegal
Everything® Guide to Being a Personal Trainer
Everything® Guide to Being a Real Estate Agent
Everything® Guide to Being a Sales Rep
Everything® Guide to Careers in Health Care
Everything® Guide to Careers in Law Enforcement
Everything® Guide to Government Jobs
Everything® Guide to Starting and Running a Restaurant
Everything® Job Interview Book
Everything® New Nurse Book
Everything® New Teacher Book
Everything® Paying for College Book
Everything® Practice Interview Book
Everything® Resume Book, 2nd Ed.
Everything® Study Book

SELF-HELP

Everything® Dating Book, 2nd Ed.
Everything® Great Sex Book
Everything® Self-Esteem Book
Everything® Tantric Sex Book

SPORTS & FITNESS

Everything® Easy Fitness Book
Everything® Running Book
Everything® Weight Training Book

TRAVEL

Everything® Family Guide to Cruise Vacations
Everything® Family Guide to Hawaii
Everything® Family Guide to Las Vegas, 2nd Ed.
Everything® Family Guide to Mexico
Everything® Family Guide to New York City, 2nd Ed.
Everything® Family Guide to RV Travel & Campgrounds
Everything® Family Guide to the Caribbean
Everything® Family Guide to the Walt Disney World Resort®, Universal Studios®, and Greater Orlando, 4th Ed.
Everything® Family Guide to Timeshares
Everything® Family Guide to Washington D.C., 2nd Ed.

WEDDINGS

Everything® Bachelorette Party Book, $9.95
Everything® Bridesmaid Book, $9.95
Everything® Destination Wedding Book
Everything® Elopement Book, $9.95
Everything® Father of the Bride Book, $9.95
Everything® Groom Book, $9.95
Everything® Mother of the Bride Book, $9.95
Everything® Outdoor Wedding Book
Everything® Wedding Book, 3rd Ed.
Everything® Wedding Checklist, $9.95
Everything® Wedding Etiquette Book, $9.95
Everything® Wedding Organizer, 2nd Ed., $16.95
Everything® Wedding Shower Book, $9.95
Everything® Wedding Vows Book, $9.95
Everything® Wedding Workout Book
Everything® Weddings on a Budget Book, $9.95

WRITING

Everything® Creative Writing Book
Everything® Get Published Book, 2nd Ed.
Everything® Grammar and Style Book
Everything® Guide to Magazine Writing
Everything® Guide to Writing a Book Proposal
Everything® Guide to Writing a Novel
Everything® Guide to Writing Children's Books
Everything® Guide to Writing Copy
Everything® Guide to Writing Research Papers
Everything® Screenwriting Book
Everything® Writing Poetry Book
Everything® Writing Well Book

Available wherever books are sold! To order, call 800-258-0929, or visit us at **www.everything.com**.
Everything® and everything.com® are registered trademarks of F+W Publications, Inc.
Bolded titles are new additions to the series.
All Everything® books are priced at $12.95 or $14.95, unless otherwise stated. Prices subject to change without notice.